Child Development for
Students in Ireland

SECOND EDITION

Child Development for Students in Ireland

SECOND EDITION

Eilis Flood

Gill & Macmillan

Gill & Macmillan
Hume Avenue
Park West
Dublin 12
with associated companies throughout the world
www.gillmacmillan.ie

978 07171 5265 2

Index compiled by Róisín Nic Cóil
Print origination in Ireland by O'K Graphic Design, Dublin
Printed by Printer Trento Srl, Italy

The paper used in this book is made from the wood pulp of managed forests. For every tree felled, at least one tree is planted, thereby renewing natural resources.

A CIP catalogue record for this book is available from the British Library.

For permission to reproduce photographs, the author and publisher gratefully acknowledge the following:

© Baby Archive: 61, 67; © Corbis: 19; © Imagefile: 75; © Lamaze: 70; © Press Association: 26; © Science Photo Library: 17, 21, 24, 151.

The author and publisher have made every effort to trace all copyright holders, but if any has been inadvertently overlooked we would be pleased to make the necessary arrangement at the first opportunity.

Contents

Preface

This book provides a comprehensive yet uncomplicated guide to child development for Irish students, particularly those studying FETAC Level 5 Child Development (5N1764) and FETAC Level 6 Child Development (6N1942). In this edition children's development from zero to six years and from six to 12 years is studied in order to fulfil the requirements for Level 6. Material additional to the new FETAC Child Development modules is included to comprehensively cover learning outcomes. There is a new chapter on the assessment requirements for both of these modules. This chapter gives both Level 5 and Level 6 students clear guidelines for completing the coursework for these two modules. Revision questions are given at the end of each chapter to help students prepare for the end-of-course examination.

Acknowledgments

I would like to express my sincere thanks to all who assisted in the production of this book. I would like to thank, as always, my husband John for his continued support and my sons Luke and Mark for their understanding while I was busy writing this book. I would like to thank everyone at Gill & Macmillan, especially Marion O'Brien, Jen Patton, Catherine Gough and Julia Fairlie.

I would also like to acknowledge my students at Drogheda Institute of Further Education, who have used the first edition of this book and given me useful feedback on it.

CHAPTER ONE

Overview of Child Development

Chapter outline

- Historical views of childhood
- Why study child development?
- The developmental process
- Developmental stages across the lifespan
- Issues in child development
- Aistear's four themes
- Revision questions

Historical views of childhood

Childhood is now considered to be such a distinct stage in life that it is difficult to imagine a time when there was little or no distinction made between it and adulthood. Children were treated as miniature adults in medieval European society and were afforded no special status. Throughout history, scholars have theorised about the length and nature of childhood and about how children should be reared. As a result, three broad philosophical views of childhood have emerged.

- **Original sin:** This view was held during the Middle Ages. Children were thought to be born as innately evil beings. The principal goal of childrearing was to rid the child of this sin, thus creating a decent, law-abiding adult. Childrearing practices were therefore harsh and punishments were severe.

- **Tabula rasa:** This view, proposed by the English philosopher John Locke (1632–1704), argued that children were not innately sinful, but instead were like a 'tabula rasa', or 'blank slate'. Locke believed that experiences in childhood were important in determining adult characteristics. He advised parents to spend time with their children (something that was not commonplace) so that they could help them to become contributing members of society. Locke and others believed that an adult's personality is largely determined by their upbringing.

Children Learn What They Live

If children live with criticism, they learn to condemn.

If children live with hostility, they learn to fight.

If children live with fear, they learn to be apprehensive.

If children live with pity, they learn to feel sorry for themselves.

If children live with ridicule, they learn to feel shy.

If children live with jealousy, they learn to feel envy.

If children live with shame, they learn to feel guilty.

If children live with encouragement, they learn confidence.

If children live with tolerance, they learn patience.

If children live with praise, they learn appreciation.

If children live with acceptance, they learn to love.

If children live with approval, they learn to like themselves.

If children live with recognition, they learn it is good to have a goal.

If children live with sharing, they learn generosity.

If children live with honesty, they learn truthfulness.

If children live with fairness, they learn justice.

If children live with kindness and consideration, they learn respect.

If children live with security, they learn to have faith in themselves and in those about them.

If children live with friendliness, they learn the world is a nice place in which to live.

Dorothy Law Nolte

- **Innate goodness:** This view, put forward by the Swiss-born philosopher Jean-Jacques Rousseau (1712–78) during the eighteenth century, stressed the inherent goodness of children. He believed that children should be allowed to grow naturally without too much parental monitoring or constraint.

Today, Western society views childhood as a highly eventful and unique period during which children master specific skills in preparation for adult life. We believe that experiences in childhood lay important foundations for adult personality and behaviour. Childhood is no longer considered to be an inconvenient waiting period during which children should be seen and not heard. Today, we protect children from adult stresses and responsibilities, we have strict child labour laws, we handle juvenile crime through a special system of juvenile justice, we have systems of child protection when families require it and we spend considerable resources researching, caring for and educating children.

Why study child development?

Over the years, the nature of childhood and child development has been the subject of much research. Why?

Improving children's health and well-being

What effects do smoking, alcohol or drug use have on the unborn foetus? How does a poor diet affect a child's ability to learn effectively? Are computer games making today's children more violent? More overweight? How environmental influences such as these affect children's mental, emotional and physical health are important to understand in order to work towards improvement, and are one of the primary reasons for studying child development.

Parenting

What effect does two parents working outside the home have on children? What difficulties may be experienced by children reared in one-parent households? Do adopted and fostered children fare as well as children raised by their biological parents? How damaging is separation and divorce to a child's development? How should children be guided and disciplined? Understanding the nature of child development can help people to become better parents. It encourages people to reflect on their own experiences as children and sort through which practices they feel were good and that they should continue, and which they feel they should adapt or abandon.

Education

How can children's overall development be best encouraged in the education setting? What method is most effective in teaching children to read and do maths? Should we be concentrating on a broad all-round education rather than focusing narrowly on academic outcomes? How can children falling behind be best identified and what interventions are most effective? How does a child's home environment affect their ability to learn effectively? What forms of behavioural management are most effective in educational settings? These are some of the questions that concern professionals working with children in an educational capacity, and are some of the reasons for much research in the area of child development.

The developmental process

We all develop similarly in some ways – for example, most full-term babies smile at six weeks, walk at about a year and say their first words at about 13 months. In other ways, however, we can develop very differently from each other. For example, some children begin reading as early as three years, whereas others may not ever learn to read fluently; some children develop great sporting talent, whereas others may show no such talent; some children show huge musical ability, whereas others do not. Child development studies the process of human development. It tries to identify its milestones and also tries to understand what best shapes and promotes it.

The pattern of human development results from an interplay between three different processes – **biological**, **cognitive** and **socio-emotional**.

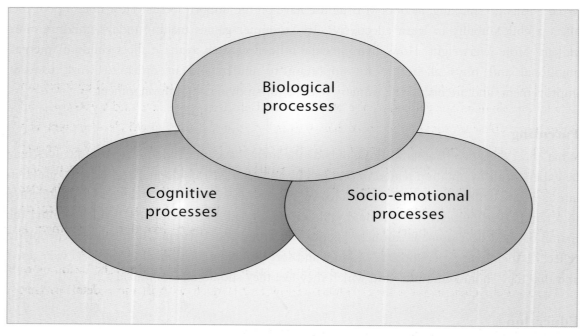

Biological, cognitive and socio-emotional processes

- **Biological processes** are responsible for physical changes that occur in the body, such as height and weight gain, hormonal changes during puberty and motor skills.
- **Cognitive processes** are responsible for changes to an individual's intelligence and language. Examples of cognitive processes are learning to string a two-word sentence together, learning to read, learning how to make a jigsaw, memorising a nursery rhyme and creating a picture.
- **Socio-emotional processes** are responsible for changes in an individual's relationships with other people, changes in their emotional state and changes in their personality, self-esteem and self-image. Examples of socio-emotional processes are an infant smiling at its mother, a child sharing their toys with a playmate or an adolescent's feelings of self-consciousness going to their first disco.

Generally these processes are closely intertwined (Diamond 2007). Take a baby laughing in response to her mother playing peek-a-boo. The baby has to be able to see what her mother is doing and use her vocal cords to laugh (biological processes). She has to understand that the mother is being playful and is doing something funny (cognitive processes). She connects with the mother in a positive way by responding appropriately to what the mother is doing, thus enriching their relationship (socio-emotional processes).

Perspectives and theories of child development (FETAC Level 6 only)

Over the years developmental theorists have proposed a number of different theories about why people develop and behave the way they do. Theorists gather data and try to come up with possible explanations for that data – thus forming a theory. Child development is a complex and multifaceted area of study. There is no one theory that covers it all. Each theory contributes a part to the overall puzzle, and while some theories seem to disagree, most complement each other in our overall understanding of how children develop. Some theories lend more weight to innate factors (heredity), while others place more importance on environment and the experiences a child has. Some theorists believe that development is continuous over the lifespan whereas others believe it occurs in distinctive stages.

Human development theory can be loosely classified under **five** different headings or perspectives. Each of these is introduced below and is dealt with in more detail in later chapters.

- **Psychoanalytic perspective** – focuses on emotions.
- **Learning perspective** – focuses on observable behaviours (sometimes called behaviourist perspective).
- **Ethological perspective** – focuses on evolutionary underpinning of behaviour (sometimes called the maturationalist perspective).
- **Cognitive perspective** – focuses on the importance of thought processes (sometimes called the constructivist perspective).
- **Contextual or social constructionist perspective** – focuses on the importance of culture and social relationships.

Psychoanalytic perspective

The psychoanalytic perspective is concerned with the unconscious forces that motivate human behaviour. This perspective was introduced at the beginning of the twentieth century with the work of Sigmund Freud, 1856–1939. Psychoanalytic theory emphasises that observable behaviour is merely a surface characteristic or manifestation of the inner workings of the mind. Psychoanalytic theorists stress the importance of early life experiences and relationships with parents in the formation of the adult personality. The psychoanalytic perspective has been expanded and modified over the years by other influential theorists, including Anna Freud, Melanie Klein, Erik Erikson, D.W. Winnicott and Jean Miller. These theorists are discussed in later chapters, particularly in Chapter 8.

Learning or behaviourist perspective

The learning or behaviourist perspective, unlike the psychoanalytic perspective, is not concerned with unconscious forces but with behaviour that can be observed and objectively studied in a scientific manner. Learning theorists believe that development results **from** learning rather than the other way round. Learning occurs when there is a long-lasting change in behaviour as a result of the individual's responding and adapting to their environment. Classical and operant conditioning are important concepts in this perspective. Ian Pavlov (1849–1936), B.F. Skinner and J.B. Watson are all important theorists of this perspective and are discussed in detail later.

Ethological or maturationalist perspective

The ethological or maturationalist perspective focuses on the biological or evolutionary basis of behaviour. This perspective originated with the famous English naturalist Charles Darwin (1809–92). In 1859 Darwin published his famous (and at the time hugely controversial) book *On the Origin of Species*. His main theses are that all species have descended over time from the same ancestors and that species-specific characteristics have evolved over time through a process of natural selection. Characteristics that are advantageous to a species' survival tend to be passed down from generation to generation, and those that are not advantageous tend not to be passed down, and die out. The Austrian ethnologists Konrad Lorenz and Karl von Frisch, together with Dutch colleague Nikolaas Tinbergen, received the Nobel Prize in Physiology or Medicine in 1973 for their observations of different species of animals both in their natural environment and in the laboratory setting. Their belief was that for each species, a variety of innate, species-specific behaviours has evolved to increase their odds of survival. In the 1950s John Bowlby extended these ethnological principles to human development with his theories on infant attachment (see Chapter 8).

Cognitive perspective

The cognitive perspective emphasises the importance of conscious thoughts and how the way we think changes as we mature. It proposes that, much like a scientist, children actively 'construct' understandings for themselves by studying the world around them. Cognitivists or constructivists do not believe that children are mere vessels to be filled with ready-made knowledge and understandings, but instead that children take in information and knowledge from the world around them, process this information and arrive at their own understandings. Jean Piaget (1896–1980) is seen as the founder of cognitive theory. His theories are dealt with in more detail in Chapters 5 and 7.

Contextual or social constructionist perspective

Like Piaget, the Russian psychologist Lev Vygotsky (1896–1934) argued that children actively construct their own knowledge. Unlike Piaget, however, he emphasised the importance of social interactions and culture to their constructions. This is why Vygotsky's theories are sometimes classified under a separate heading from Piaget's, namely **social constructionism**. Vygotsky's theories are dealt with in more detail in Chapter 5.

Developmental stages across the lifespan

While this book deals primarily with children's development between zero and 12 years of age, we look briefly here at where this period fits within the overall lifespan development.

Periods of development

- **The prenatal period** covers the time from conception to birth (approximately 40 weeks). Some people believe that it should also include the months leading up to conception, when factors such as the mother's folic acid intake, diet and lifestyle can affect the baby's development. The prenatal period is critical for all others.
- **The infancy period** generally covers the time from birth to two years. While the infancy period is characterised by a dependence on adults, it is also a period of intense growth and development. During this period, babies learn to sit up, crawl, walk, run, smile, laugh and begin to talk.
- **The early childhood period** generally covers years two to six and is sometimes referred to as the pre-school years, even though in Ireland (unlike other countries) children can attend formal schooling from four years. During this period, children's development focuses on becoming more self-sufficient, e.g. toileting and feeding, on developing school readiness skills, e.g. letter recognition, and on developing relationships with others, including peers.

- **The middle to late childhood period** generally covers years six to 11, when children attend primary school. During this period, children master such skills as reading, writing and maths, becoming more exposed to the world outside their immediate environment. Achievement becomes important to children at this stage and self-control increases.

- **The adolescent period** generally covers years 11 to 19. Adolescence begins with rapid physical changes, such as dramatic increases in height, weight and shape, as well as sexual maturation. The pursuit of a stable identity is one of the main tasks of adolescence. The peer group becomes increasingly important. Thinking becomes more abstract and idealistic, while at the same time more logical.

Developmental psychologists such as Levinson (1978) no longer believe that development ceases at adolescence, but instead have identified a further three developmental periods – early adulthood (19–40), middle adulthood (40–65) and late adulthood (65+). Like earlier periods during childhood, each of these stages has their its developmental targets.

Issues in child development

While there has been a huge volume of research carried out on all aspects of child development, there are a number of issues on which there is continued disagreement. Three such issues or debates are examined here: nature vs. nurture, early vs. later experiences and continuity vs. discontinuity.

Nature vs. nurture debate

The nature vs. nurture debate has long been the subject of discussion among developmental psychologists. The debate centres on the question of whether development is primarily influenced by nature (genetics) or by nurture (environment). Almost nobody argues today that development can be explained by either nature or nurture alone. However, which is more important? This is where disagreement arises.

Twin studies have been used to investigate this issue further. For example, in 1979, Thomas Bouchard began to study identical twins separated at birth and raised in different families. He found that an identical twin reared away from his or her co-twin has an equal chance of being similar to the co-twin in terms of personality, interests and attitudes as one who has been reared with his or her co-twin. This leads to the conclusion that the similarities between twins are due to genes, not environment, and that the differences between twins reared apart must be due totally to the environment.

THE TWO JIMS

Jim Lewis and Jim Springer are one set of a number of American identical twins studied by Dr Thomas Bouchard. The two Jims first met aged 39 after being separated at four weeks old. Both had been named James by their adoptive parents. Both were married twice, first to women named Linda and then to women named Betty. Both had children, including sons named James Alan. Both had at one time owned dogs named Toy. Each twin went to the same place on holiday, smoked Salem cigarettes, drank Miller Lite beer, were nail biters and had at one time held part-time posts as sheriffs.

Dr Thomas Bouchard (1990) and his colleagues studied the personalities and attitudes of the twin Jims, and the resulting similarities were again astonishing. In one test measuring personality traits, the twins' scores were as close as would be expected from one person taking the test twice. Brain wave tests were almost identical. Intelligence tests, mental abilities, gestures, voice tones, likes and dislikes were all very similar as well. So were medical histories: both had high blood pressure, both had experienced what they thought were heart attacks, both had undergone vasectomies and both suffered from migraine headaches.

In contrast, other psychologists emphasise the importance of nurture, or environmental experiences, to development (Maccoby 2007). Experiences can mean the individual's biological environment (nutrition, medical care, use of drugs and other substances, physical accidents) or their social environment (family, peers, school, work, community, the media and their culture). For example, contrast two children with similar genetic wiring – one from a stable, two-parent middle-class family with nutritious meals, lots of books and other educational material at home, regular family holidays abroad and lots of hobbies that are encouraged and supported, and another from a lone-parent family surviving on welfare with a poor diet, few books at home, no family holidays and few hobbies. While both children have the same genetic potential, they are likely to grow up quite differently.

Early vs. later experiences debate

The early vs. later experiences debate centres on the degree to which early experiences (especially in infancy) or later experiences influence a child's long-term development. People in Western cultures, particularly those influenced by Freudian theory, tend to place great importance on early experiences, believing that an infant's first experiences of the world in some ways form a blueprint for all other experiences. In contrast, those who advocate the importance of later experiences argue that children are malleable throughout development and that care and sensitivity, or indeed neglect, in later life can override early negative or positive experiences.

CASE STUDY

When Danielle Holden had her first child, Barry, at 19 years of age, she was not in a good place. She was not in a stable relationship with the baby's father, who was unemployed and a heavy drinker who was abusive when drunk. On a number of occasions they had huge arguments in front of the baby. She was living in a small rented flat that had dampness, poor light and poor ventilation. Danielle worked at a part-time cleaning job to supplement her welfare payments and so had to ask favours off friends and family to mind Barry while she worked. Danielle smoked heavily and on occasions also drank heavily. She did not take any exams at school, leaving in 2nd year. While Danielle was patient with Barry most of the time, she did sometimes get angry with him when he would not stop crying. On a few occasions she treated him roughly, shaking and shouting at him in frustration.

Life went on like this until Barry was two years old. Then, as a result of a government back-to-education initiative, Danielle returned to education, starting a one-year FETAC-certified childcare course. While attending the course, Barry was cared for in a community crèche. In the crèche, however, Barry was experiencing difficulties. Staff became concerned about his aggressive behaviour – he frequently bit and hit other children. He also had a lot of health problems, with asthma and frequent chest and ear infections. While on the course, Danielle learned a lot about child development and caring for children. As a result, she stopped smoking around Barry and started spending time doing activities with him.

Do you think Barry's early negative experiences will influence his overall development?

Continuity vs. discontinuity debate

The continuity vs. discontinuity debate centres on the extent to which development involves slow, gradual change (continuity) or distinct stages (discontinuity). The continuity vs. discontinuity debate is linked with nature vs. nurture in that some psychologists, such as Piaget (see p. 102), believe our development is biologically determined and occurs in distinctive stages, whereas others, such as Vygotsky (see p. 110), see development as inseparable from social and cultural activities, and that it is continuous and gradual in nature.

Aistear's four themes

Aistear is the **National Curriculum Framework** for children from birth to six years in Ireland. Aistear was developed by the National Council for Curriculum and Assessment (NCCA) in partnership with the early childhood sector in Ireland and abroad and was published in 2008.

The Aistear curriculum is organised around four themes:

1. Well-being
2. Identity and belonging
3. Communicating
4. Exploring and thinking

These themes promote children's holistic development. Aistear breaks each theme down into four aims, each of which is broken down into six learning goals.

Here is an example of one aim and its accompanying six learning goals under the theme Identity and belonging:

Identity and belonging	
Aims	**Learning goals**
Aim 1: Children will have strong self-identities and will feel respected and affirmed as unique individuals with their own life stories.	In partnership with the adult, children will: 1. build respectful relationships with others 2. appreciate the features that make a person special and unique (name, size, hair, hand and footprint, gender, birthday) 3. understand that as individuals they are separate from others with their own needs, interests and abilities 4. have a sense of 'who they are' and be able to describe their backgrounds, strengths and abilities 5. feel valued and see themselves and their interests reflected in the environment 6. express their own ideas, preferences and needs, and have these responded to with respect and consistency.

Aistear then gives the early years practitioner examples of **learning experiences** that work towards fulfilling these aims and learning goals.

Revision questions

1. What are the three broad philosophical views of childhood?
2. List three reasons why it is important to study child development.
3. The pattern of human development results from an interplay between three different processes – what are they?
4. Human development theory can be loosely classified under five different headings or perspectives. Name and briefly describe each of the five perspectives. (FETAC Level 6 only)
5. List Levinson's eight periods of development.
6. What is meant by the nature vs. nurture debate?
7. What is meant by the early vs. later experiences debate? What is your opinion?
8. What is meant by the continuity vs. discontinuity debate?
9. What is Aistear and what are its four themes?

Prenatal Development and Birth

Genetic foundations of development

Each of us begins life as a single cell weighing about one-millionth of a gram. This tiny cell contains our entire genetic code, or blueprint, reproducing itself many millions of times in order to create the person you are.

The nucleus of each human cell contains **chromosomes**, which are thread-like structures made up of deoxyribonucleic acid (**DNA**). **Genes** are short segments or pieces of DNA that contain all the hereditary information about an individual, e.g. eye and hair colour, height, intelligence. In addition, some life-threatening conditions are genetically transmitted, e.g. cystic fibrosis.

Each gene has a specific location on a particular chromosome. Scientists have long tried to discover where specific genes are located in order to help prevent genetically transmitted conditions. In total, humans are now thought to have approximately 20,500 genes, many of which contribute to the same function, e.g. athletic ability. It is also thought that the activity of many genes can be either turned 'on' or 'off' by the environment in which the individual is living – thus, a child born with a powerful genetic literary ability may have their ability 'turned off' by an environment were the child is not exposed to books.

Genetic reproduction

All cells in your body, with the exception of the sperm and egg, contain 46 chromosomes. These cells reproduce by a process called **mitosis**. During mitosis, the cell's nucleus (which contains the chromosomes) duplicates itself and the cell divides, forming two new cells. Each of the two new cells contains the same DNA as the original cell and will go on to duplicate in the same way.

However, a different type of cell division, called **meiosis**, occurs to form eggs and sperm (gametes). During meiosis, a cell of the testes (in males) or ovaries (in females) duplicates its chromosomes but then divides twice, forming four cells, each of which has only 23 unpaired chromosomes.

During **fertilisation,** an egg (containing 23 unpaired chromosomes) and a sperm (also containing 23 unpaired chromosomes) join to create a single cell with 46 chromosomes (23 pairs). Male and female babies differ in that in females, the twenty-third pair is made up of two large X chromosomes (XX), whereas in males, the twenty-third pair is made up of one large X chromosome and one smaller Y chromosome (XY).

Genotype and phenotype

All of us get genetic material from both our parents. This is called our **genotype**. However, not all genetic material 'comes out' in the individual. For example, a child may have a blue-eyed mother and a brown-eyed father, so both blue eyes and brown eyes are part of their genotype. If they actually have brown eyes, then while blue eyes are part of their genotype, it is not part of their **phenotype** (the characteristics that actually come through). Phenotypes include **physical characteristics,** such as hair and eye colour, height and foot size, as well as **psychological characteristics,** such as personality and intelligence. In addition, sometimes how the phenotype emerges depends on environmental factors, e.g. a person who is genetically predisposed to putting on excessive weight may prevent this trait from coming out as their phenotype through good nutrition and lots of exercise.

Genetic principles

There are a number of genetic principles (apart from environmental factors, as mentioned above) that determine how a genotype is expressed to create a specific phenotype. While many of these are still unclear, some have been more widely researched and are therefore more fully understood.

Dominant-recessive gene principle

In some gene pairs, one gene is 'stronger' than the other. The 'stronger' gene is called the **dominant gene** and the 'weaker' one is called **recessive.** When a recessive gene and a dominant gene form the genotype, the dominant gene always comes out in the phenotype. This is called the dominant-recessive gene principle. Recessive genes only come out in the phenotype if they are inherited from both parents.

	Dominant traits	**Recessive traits**
Eye colour	Brown	Grey, green, hazel, blue
Vision	Long-sightedness Normal vision Normal vision	Normal vision Short-sightedness Colour blindness
Hair	Dark hair Curly hair Full head of hair Widow's peak	Blonde, red hair Straight hair Baldness Normal hairline
Facial features	Dimples Unattached earlobes Freckles Broad lips	No dimples Attached earlobes No freckles Thin lips
Other	Double jointed Immune to poison ivy Normal pigmented skin Normal blood clotting Normal hearing No PKU	Not double jointed Susceptible to poison ivy Albinism Haemophilia Congenital deafness Phenylketonuria (PKU)

Question: Elaine and Peter Jones, who each have normal sight (NS), have four children. Three of the children have normal sight, whereas their eldest child, Eoin, is short-sighted (SS). Look at the table above and write out Elaine, Peter and Eoin's genotype for vision.

Sex-linked gene principle

Most mutated genes, e.g. the gene for both cystic fibrosis and sickle cell anaemia, are recessive. This means that you must have inherited the gene from both parents to actually suffer the symptoms of the condition. However, if a mutated gene is carried on the X chromosome, this will have more serious consequences for boys than for girls, since boys have only one X chromosome. If a disease-causing gene is carried on the X chromosome, boys will not have another healthy X chromosome to balance things out and may therefore suffer from the condition, even if it is recessive. Girls, on the other hand, have a second X chromosome, which is unlikely to also carry the condition. Thus, while girls may act as **carriers** of the disease, they are unlikely to actually have the disease. Haemophilia and fragile X syndrome (see the next section) are examples of X-linked inherited diseases.

Genetic imprinting principle

As you know, half of an individual's genes are inherited from their mother and half from their father. Genetic imprinting occurs when a chemical process in the body 'silences' one half of a gene pair. Sometimes the maternal gene is silenced and other times the paternal gene is silenced. Genetic imprinting only occurs with a small number of gene pairs. Most gene pairs do not follow this principle, but rather the dominant-recessive gene principle described earlier. If genetic imprinting does not occur when it should, development is disturbed. Wilms' tumour or Beckwith-Wiedemann syndrome, a condition whereby children overgrow and are prone to childhood cancers, are examples of conditions resulting from a failure of genetic imprinting.

Polygenic inheritance principle

The principle of polygenic inheritance states that few characteristics are influenced by a single gene or pair of genes. Most characteristics involve many different genes. This makes dealing with genetically transmitted disorders even more complex.

Chromosomal and gene-linked abnormalities

Sometimes the process of genetic transmission results in abnormalities. Some of these abnormalities involve whole chromosomes, while others just involve harmful genes present on an otherwise normal chromosome.

Chromosomal abnormalities

Down's syndrome

It is believed that people with Down's syndrome have always existed. However, it was not until 1866 that the English doctor John Langdon Down first described the condition, which subsequently took his name. It was first understood as a chromosomal abnormality in 1959 when Professor Jérôme Lejeune, a Parisian geneticist, discovered that Down's syndrome occurred as a result of a trisomy of chromosome 21. This means that instead of the usual 46 chromosomes in the cells of the body, there is an extra chromosome 21, making 47 chromosomes in all. Since then, other forms of the condition, which are much rarer, have been discovered, such as translocation (where one parent passes on an abnormal rather than an extra chromosome 21 which contains extra material) and mosaicism (where some cells in the body have the normal 46 chromosomes, while others have 47). Approximately 94 per cent of people with Down's syndrome have standard trisomy 21, 4 per cent have a translocation and 2 per cent have mosaic Down's syndrome. Individuals with mosaic Down's syndrome may show fewer or less severe symptoms of the condition, depending on what percentage of their body cells have 47 chromosomes.

Individuals with Down's syndrome have a number of distinctive physical characteristics, such as a small mouth, which is often kept open because of their large tongue and high arched palate. They will have a flat nasal bridge, low hairline and small, low-set ears. Eyes characteristically slant upwards and outwards, with extra skin folds on the upper and lower lids. Hands will be characteristically broad, with short fingers, and there may be only one palm crease. Feet will be broad and short with a deep cleft between the first and second toe. Individuals will also have intellectual disabilities and may have other health-related problems,

Child with mosaic Down's syndrome

such as frequent ear and chest infections due to a weaker immune system, poor vision and heart problems. Down's syndrome is extremely rare among black children.

On average, Down's syndrome appears approximately once in every 700 live births but more frequently as maternal age progresses (see table below). It is not known why this is the case. Many women, particularly those over the age of 35, opt to have prenatal diagnostic tests done (see the next section) to detect Down's syndrome and other genetic abnormalities; this practice is understandably controversial.

Maternal age	Risk
15–19	1 in 1,850
20–25	1 in 1,400
26–30	1 in 800
31–35	1 in 380
36–40	1 in 190
41–45	1 in 110
45+	1 in 30

Sex-linked chromosomal abnormalities

A newborn normally has either two X chromosomes (girl) or an X and a Y chromosome (boy). The most common sex-linked chromosomal abnormalities involve either the presence of an extra chromosome (X or Y) or the absence of one X chromosome in females.

- **Fragile X syndrome** occurs in approximately one in 2,000 males. While many girls (one in approximately 250) have an affected X chromosome, they rarely show symptoms of the condition because of their second X chromosome, which counteracts the effect. Fragile X occurs as a result of the X chromosome being constricted or broken. Boys with fragile X may show physically distinctive traits, e.g. long face, prominent ears, long fingers with double-jointed thumbs, flat feet, larger than normal testicles and poor muscle tone. Usually they will also have intellectual disabilities, a short attention span and poor memory and social skills.

- **Klinefelter's syndrome** occurs when males have an extra X chromosome, making them XXY rather than XY. It is estimated that while one in every 500 males has the syndrome, only one in every 1,000 exhibits symptoms. Males with this condition are usually very tall, will have an underdeveloped penis and testes, resulting in infertility, and may have increased breast tissue. In addition, there is frequently language and intellectual impairment with poor motor co-ordination.

- **XYY Syndrome** (sometimes called Jacob's syndrome) occurs in approximately one in every 1,000 males. Males with the condition have an additional Y chromosome resulting in 47 chromosomes in each body cell. XYY males tend to be taller than expected (taking parents' height into consideration) and some studies show reduced IQ levels when compared with non-XYY siblings. This condition has for many years been associated with an aggressive criminal personality. Many of these studies have since, however, been criticised due to their method of studying height-selected, institutionalised males. (FETAC Level 6 only)

- **Turner syndrome** occurs approximately once in every 2,500 females. The condition occurs when there is only one full X chromosome present. The X chromosome may not be absent from all cells, so in this way there can be degrees of Turner syndrome. Common symptoms include short stature, oedema (swelling) of the hands and feet, a broad chest (shield chest) and widely spaced nipples, low hairline, low-set ears, infertility due to underdeveloped ovaries, absence of a menstrual period, obesity, shortened fourth finger, small fingernails, webbed neck, heart defects, poor breast development, kidney problems, visual impairment, ear infections and hearing loss.

Gene-linked abnormalities

Abnormalities can be produced not only by an abnormal number of chromosomes, but also by harmful genes on chromosomes. Most harmful genes are recessive and are very rare.

Sickle cell anaemia

Sickle cell anaemia is a genetically inherited life-threatening condition that affects red blood cells. Sickle cell anaemia mainly affects black people living in or originating from sub-Saharan Africa, but it is also less commonly found among Greeks, Indians, Italians, Saudi Arabians, South Americans and Turks. The reason for this distribution is thought to be because sickle cell carriers are resistant to malaria, so is an adaptive trait in countries with malaria. Prevalence of the disease varies from country to country. In Nigeria, for example, 24 per cent of the population are carriers of the mutant gene and the prevalence of sickle cell anaemia is about one per 50 births. This means that in Nigeria alone, more than 100,000 children are born annually with sickle cell anaemia (WHO 2005).

Someone with sickle cell anaemia produces abnormal 'sickle'-shaped red blood cells, which are inefficient oxygen carriers and have a tendency to clump together in the blood vessels, causing very painful episodes called 'crises'. Sickle cell anaemia also causes organ damage, particularly to the spleen and kidneys, and may cause stroke. While some children with sickle cell anaemia do not make it through childhood, there are an increasing number of treatments available that help treat the symptoms of the disease. As a result, more and more people, particularly in developed countries such as America, are living long and healthy lives.

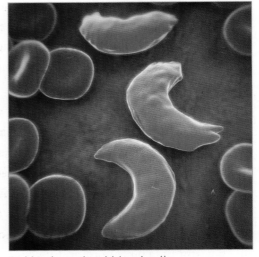

Sickle-shaped red blood cells

People with sickle cell anaemia may be on a special diet and given daily doses of folic acid and penicillin. They may get frequent blood transfusions and some have had bone marrow transplants in order to help the condition. When a crisis occurs, pain management medication such as morphine is given, which may require hospitalisation.

Cystic fibrosis

Cystic fibrosis (CF) is Ireland's most common life-threatening genetically inherited disease. Currently there are more than a thousand people suffering from CF in Ireland, the highest proportion per head of population in the world. Approximately 1 in 19 Irish people are carriers of the CF gene, and where two carriers parent a child together, there is a one in four chance of the baby being born with CF.

CF affects the glands of the body, damaging many organs, including the lungs, pancreas, digestive tract and reproductive system. It causes a thick, sticky mucus to be produced, blocking the bronchial tubes of the lungs and preventing the body's natural enzymes from digesting food. As a result, people with CF are prone to constant lung infections and malnutrition.

At birth, some babies with CF will present with a bowel obstruction and will not pass their first dark stool (meconium). This is why hospitals ask mothers to keep their baby's first dirty nappy for inspection. Babies who are suspected of having CF are then given further tests to confirm a diagnosis.

The symptoms of CF are chronic or recurrent respiratory symptoms such as a cough or wheeze and pneumonia. Children will fail to thrive despite normal appetite. They may have malformed, bulky, offensive stools with an oily appearance and chronic diarrhoea. A rectal prolapse may also occur. Skin will taste salty and there may be prolonged jaundice in infants.

Treatment for CF includes the use of nebulisers and antibiotics to help breathing and control lung infections, daily physiotherapy to loosen mucus and nutritional supplements. Many people with CF are awaiting lung transplant operations, which significantly prolong life. The main centre for the treatment of CF in Ireland is St Vincent's Hospital, Elm Park, Dublin.

Spina bifida

Spina bifida is a relatively common condition, affecting about one in every 1,000 babies born per year in Ireland. Ireland has one of the highest incidences of spina bifida births in the world. Spina bifida is the most common neural tube defect, which causes incomplete development of the spinal cord. Translated, it literally means 'split spine'.

The spine is made up of separate bones called vertebrae, which normally cover and protect the spinal cord. With spina bifida, some of these vertebrae are not completely formed. Instead, they are split and the spinal cord and its coverings usually protrude through a sac-like bulge on the back, covered with a thin membrane. The degree of disability experienced depends on how much of the spinal cord is protruding, where it is protruding and how much damage has been done to the nerves. The vast majority of neural tube defects arise as a result of the interaction between susceptible genes and some environmental trigger. Which particular genes make a couple susceptible to having an affected child is not yet fully understood.

A child with spina bifida

At least one outside trigger is now well known: folic acid (vitamin B complex) has proved to be an extremely important factor. It is now known that women who take daily folic acid supplements or multivitamins containing at least 400 mg of folic acid both before conception and for the first 12 weeks after conception reduce their chances of having a baby with spina bifida by approximately 75 per cent.

There are at least five different forms of spina bifida, the most common of which is **myelomeningocele** (pronounced my-lo-men-in-jo-seal). The split normally occurs in the lumbar region, and as a result, there is usually some degree of paralysis and loss of sensation from this region down.

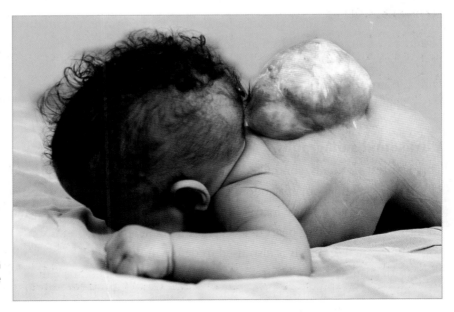

Baby with spina bifida myelomeningocele before surgery

Phenylketonuria (PKU)

Phenylketonuria, or PKU, is a genetic disorder in which the individual cannot properly metabolise (break down) the amino acid phenylalanine (found in protein foods, including breast milk). If undetected, phenylalanine builds up in the system, causing brain damage. PKU results from a recessive gene and occurs in approximately one in 15,000 births worldwide. Ireland has a much higher incidence of the condition, at one in 4,500 births. PKU is detected in newborns using the 'heel prick' test, and if found, the infant will be put on a phenylalanine-free diet. The child will continue to follow this diet throughout their life – foods such as meat, chicken, fish, cheese, milk, nuts, legumes and some cereals must all be eliminated. The artificial sweetener aspartame must also be avoided. Some medications, e.g. Kuvan, are also used.

Other diseases

Other diseases that result from genetic abnormalities include diabetes, haemophilia, Huntington's disease and Tay-Sachs disease. In addition, research such as the Human Genome Project in the US has identified a number of different conditions with genetic links, such as Alzheimer's disease, asthma, cancer and hypertension.

Diagnostic testing

One choice open to prospective parents is prenatal diagnostic testing. A number of tests can now be carried out while the foetus is still in the womb, which can indicate whether a foetus is developing normally. Such tests include ultrasound, MRI scanning, chorionic villus sampling, amniocentesis and maternal blood screening. Such testing raises ethical questions, however, in that couples may decide to abort a foetus that tests positive for certain conditions. Also, in some countries where male children are sought after, female foetuses have been known to be aborted. However, testing does allow timely medical and surgical treatments to be carried out on babies with certain conditions and gives parents of the baby time to prepare psychologically, socially and financially for the birth of a baby with special needs.

Ultrasound sonography

This is a test normally conducted early in pregnancy. High-frequency sound waves are directed into the pregnant woman's abdomen and the echo from these sound waves transforms into a visual representation of the foetus's inner structures. Ultrasound can detect a number of structural abnormalities, including heart defects and microencephaly, a condition whereby the foetus has an abnormally small brain. It is also used to detect multiple pregnancies (twins or more) and can be used to determine the baby's sex. Nowadays detailed 3-D scans can be performed giving a very clear picture of the foetus. This technology can be used to detect conditions such as spina bifida.

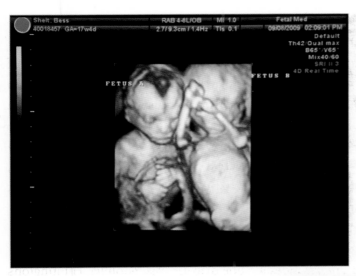

Very detailed 3-D ultrasound scan

A woman having an ultrasound scan

Foetal MRI

Foetal MRI uses what is called magnetic resonance imaging, resulting in a more detailed image than is possible with ultrasound. Foetal MRIs are normally conducted only if the results of the ultrasound suggest an abnormality.

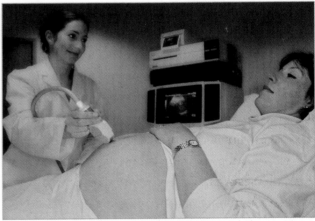

Chorionic villus sampling

This test is usually conducted between the tenth and twelfth week of pregnancy, when a sample of cells is taken from the placenta and sent away for testing. This is an invasive testing technique and carries with it a small risk of miscarriage (1 per cent). It can detect with a large degree of accuracy the presence of a range of genetic conditions, e.g. Down's syndrome, cystic fibrosis, PKU and sickle cell anaemia.

Amniocentesis

This test is usually conducted between the fifteenth and eighteenth week of pregnancy, when a sample of amniotic fluid is withdrawn using a fine needle and sent away for testing. Like chorionic villus sampling, this is an invasive testing technique and carries with it a small risk of miscarriage (0.5 per cent). Like chorionic villus sampling, it can detect with a large degree of accuracy the presence of a range of genetic conditions.

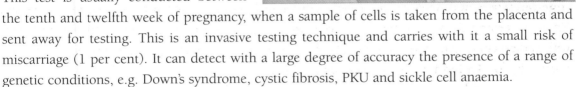

Maternal blood screening

This test can be conducted on a sample of the mother's blood from the sixteenth week onwards. Unlike chorionic villus sampling and amniocentesis, non-invasive blood tests such as this cannot diagnose a birth defect – they can only indicate that there may be one. Certain conditions in the foetus, such as Down's syndrome and spina bifida, cause an increase in certain substances in the mother's blood. Detecting these raised amounts is how a positive screen result is obtained.

Infertility and reproductive technology

It is estimated that approximately one in seven couples experiences fertility problems. There are many reasons for infertility – ovulation problems, blockage of fallopian tubes, low sperm count or poor sperm motility, age-related factors, problems of the uterine lining, previous tubal ligation, previous vasectomy, tuberculosis (TB) or cystic fibrosis. Sometimes, however, the cause is unexplained.

Nowadays, with increased understanding and availability of reproductive technologies, many couples undergo assistive conception treatments every year. The most common technique is in vitro fertilisation (IVF), whereby the woman is given hormones to encourage the production of a number of eggs. These are removed from the ovaries and fertilised using her partner's sperm (or donor sperm) in a special culture. If eggs successfully fertilise and divide, one or two are then returned to the woman's uterus, where they will hopefully implant and result in pregnancy. Extra embryos are normally frozen for future cycles.

Conception to birth

Prenatal development lasts approximately 40 weeks, beginning with fertilisation and ending with birth. It can generally be divided into three different stages – germinal, embryonic and foetal.

The germinal stage

The germinal stage takes place during the first two weeks after conception. During this stage, the cells of the fertilised egg (called the zygote) divide continuously, attaching to the uterine wall. Approximately one week after conception, a group of cells, called the **blastocyst**, has formed. The inner mass of these cells will become the embryo and the outer layer, called the **trophoblast**, becomes the placenta and umbilical cord. Ten to 14 days after conception, the zygote attaches itself to the wall of the uterus; this is called **implantation.** Once implantation begins, a hormone called human chorionic gonadotropin (hCG) is released. This is the hormone detected by pregnancy test kits.

The embryonic stage

The embryonic stage is the period from two to eight weeks after conception. The zygote is called an embryo from two weeks. During this time, the cells of the embryo differentiate or organise themselves into three different layers – the **endoderm**, **mesoderm** and **ectoderm**. The endoderm is the innermost layer and will become the innermost organs of the body – the digestive and respiratory systems. The middle layer (mesoderm) will form the circulatory, excretory and reproductive systems along with the bones and muscles. The outer ectoderm will form the nervous system, ears, nose, eyes, skin, hair and nails. This process of organ formation is called **organogenesis**. It is a critical period of development, during which the embryo can be seriously harmed by **teratogens** (harmful substances such as alcohol).

As the embryo cells begin to differentiate, its life-support system also develops. This life-support system includes the **amniotic sac (amnion)**, **umbilical cord** and **placenta.** The amniotic sac is a bag filled with fluid (called amniotic fluid) that provides a constant temperature and shockproof environment for the developing embryo. The umbilical cord contains two arteries and one vein and connects the embryo to the placenta. The placenta consists of a disc-shaped mass of tissue, in which tiny blood vessels (capillaries) of the mother and embryo intertwine but do not mix. Because the blood vessels of the mother and embryo lie so close to each other, food and oxygen can pass from mother to embryo and waste products from embryo to mother. This continues throughout the pregnancy. Unfortunately, some harmful substances, e.g. heroin, are also small enough to pass across.

At the end of this stage, the embryo is about 2.5 centimetres (1 inch) long and weighs about 1 gram.

The foetal stage

This stage begins two months after conception and ends at birth. The embryo is now called a foetus. During this time, the foetus continues to grow and develop rapidly. By three months, the foetus has tripled in size and now weighs about 75 grams. During the fourth month, the lower body begins to grow and the mother begins to feel movements as the foetus kicks and moves its arms and legs. By the end of the fifth month, the foetus is approximately 30 centimetres long (1 foot) and will weigh up to 500 grams (1 pound). The skin and nails will form. The foetus is very active at this stage and normally shows a preference for a particular position in the womb.

By six months, the foetus will be approximately 35 centimetres (14 inches) long and will have gained another 250 to 500 grams (1/2 to 1 pound). The eyes and eyelids will have fully formed and there will be a covering of fine hair over the head and parts of the body. From seven months, the foetus would have a good chance of survival if born prematurely, although babies born at this stage will need help breathing and may suffer long-term physical, intellectual and emotional effects. By the end of the seventh month, the foetus is approximately 40 centimetres (16 inches) long and weighs 1,500 grams (3 pounds).

During the last two months in the womb, the foetus puts on fatty tissue and organs such as the kidneys, heart and lungs (last) develop more fully. At birth, the average baby weighs 3.4 kilograms (7 1/2 pounds) and is 50 centimetres (20 inches) long.

Sometimes a pregnancy is divided into three **trimesters** – this is different from the three stages described above. Each trimester lasts three months and viability (the chance of surviving outside the womb) occurs at the beginning of the third trimester.

Development of the nervous system

The basic structure of the human nervous system – that is, the brain, spinal cord and nerve cells, or **neurons** – is formed during the first two trimesters of prenatal development. During the final trimester of prenatal development and the first two years of life, the focus is on the development of connections within the system.

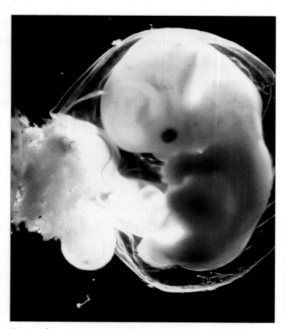

An embryo at six weeks

During the first three weeks after conception, the nervous system begins forming as a long, hollow tube along the embryo's back. Normally this tube closes approximately 24 days after conception. Spina bifida occurs when the neural tube fails to close over, leaving the spinal cord exposed. Once the tube closes, the embryo begins reproducing millions of nerve cells, or neurons, daily. This process is called **neurogenesis.** As the pregnancy progresses, the nervous system becomes more organised and mature.

Teratology

Teratology is the name given to the study of the causes of birth defects. A **teratogen** is anything that can potentially cause a birth defect or negatively affect any area of development. Teratogens include drugs, infectious diseases, advanced maternal or paternal age, environmental pollutants, incompatible blood types (one parent having Rhesus-negative blood and the other positive) and nutritional deficiencies. Exposure to teratogens during the germinal period will normally prevent implantation, so pregnancy will frequently not occur. If the pregnancy does continue, teratogens generally have the most damaging effects if exposure occurs during the embryonic stage (two to eight weeks after conception). As stated earlier, this is when organogenesis occurs and therefore structural damage to the organs may occur. Exposure during the foetal stage normally causes stunted growth and problems with organ function.

Prescription and non-prescription drugs

Prescription drugs such as the antibiotic Streptomycin, found to cause deafness, and Accutane, a drug given to treat acne and which has been found to cause brain, heart and facial defects, should be completely avoided during pregnancy. Non-prescription drugs that can be harmful include slimming tablets and aspirin. To be safe, women who suspect they may be pregnant should not take any form of medication without first consulting their doctor.

Psychoactive drugs

Psychoactive drugs are drugs that act on the nervous system, causing changes to the individual's physical and mental state. Examples of psychoactive drugs include caffeine, alcohol, nicotine, marijuana, cocaine and heroin.

Caffeine

Caffeine is found in tea, coffee, chocolate, cola and other soft drinks, e.g. Red Bull. Studies have found that caffeine intakes in excess of 200 milligrams (two cups of tea or coffee) increase the risk of miscarriage and low birth weight. Pregnant women should therefore avoid caffeine or consume very little.

Alcohol

Alcohol consumption by women during pregnancy can have devastating effects on their children. Foetal alcohol spectrum disorders (FASDs), sometimes referred to as foetal alcohol syndrome (FAS), are a cluster of abnormalities and problems that appear in the offspring of mothers who drink alcohol during pregnancy. Effects of the condition vary from child to child but include:

- Facial abnormalities such as wide-set eyes, thin upper lip, flat cheekbones and unevenly paired ears.
- Heart defects.
- Limb defects, particularly of the right hand and forearm.
- Learning problems – many have below-average IQ and a significant number have severe learning difficulties.
- Impaired memory functioning.

- Increased incidence of attention deficit and hyperactivity disorder (ADHD).
- The children will be prone to addiction themselves.
- Prone to depression and other psychiatric illnesses.
- A large proportion grow up to become unemployed, with many unable to live independently (Spohr, Williams and Steinhausen 2007).

A child with foetal alcohol syndrome

It is recommended that no alcohol is consumed during pregnancy. While moderate drinking is unlikely to cause FASDs, some studies have shown that it increases the risk of premature birth. Other studies have found that the children of women who drink moderately during pregnancy are smaller and less attentive and alert than the children of women who do not drink at all (Pollard 2007).

Nicotine

Smoking cigarettes during pregnancy increases the risk of the baby being preterm and low birth weight, foetal death, respiratory problems and sudden infant death syndrome (SIDS). Studies also link smoking during pregnancy and increased irritability, lower scores on cognitive tests and increased inattention in children (Van Meurs 1999). Others argue that such differences could be due to other environmental factors as well as smoking. Women who quit smoking during early pregnancy can avoid these problems, thereby reducing the risk to their baby to that of the level of a non-smoker.

Marijuana

There have been a number of longitudinal studies carried out into the effects of marijuana use during pregnancy. Effects include reduced intelligence, memory and information-processing skills as well as increased childhood depression and early marijuana use by the child themselves (Fried and Smith 2001). Marijuana should not be used in pregnancy.

Cocaine

Cocaine use during pregnancy can cause a myriad of negative effects in children, such as low birth weight and head circumference, prematurity, higher excitability and irritability, slower motor development, slower growth rate, increased risk of ADHD and learning difficulties and impaired language development. Some researchers suggest that these results be viewed with caution, as it is also more likely that mothers who use cocaine also live in poverty, are badly nourished and use other harmful substances such as alcohol, nicotine, marijuana and other drugs.

Heroin

Babies born to heroin users and users of the heroin substitute methadone are likely to experience withdrawal symptoms such as tremors, poor sleep patterns, irritability and shrill crying. 'Heroin babies' are more likely to have ADHD and experience behavioural problems as they get older. There is also the possibility of HIV infection being passed on as a result of using dirty needles.

Blood incompatibility

Everyone is born with a specific blood type and Rhesus (Rh) factor. The four different blood groups are A, B, AB or O, and the Rhesus factor is either Rh-negative or Rh-positive. Most people are Rh-positive, with approximately 15 per cent of white people Rh-negative (Rh-negative blood is much less common among black and Asian populations, at approximately 5 per cent). Blood incompatibility can arise if the mother is Rh-negative and her baby is Rh-positive. This is because the mother's body may begin to produce anti-Rh-positive antibodies that can pass across the placenta and harm the baby. This does not usually happen on the first pregnancy, but if the baby's and mother's blood mix during labour and birth (which they are likely to do), the mother may then begin producing anti-Rh-positive antibodies that would attack any subsequent Rh-positive baby. Straight after birth, a sample of blood from the baby's umbilical cord will be tested to determine whether the baby is Rh-positive or negative. In addition, a sample of the mother's blood will be taken to determine the number of foetal blood cells present in her own blood. If foetal cells are found and the baby is Rh-positive, then the mother will be given an anti-D injection that will prevent her from developing anti-Rh-positive antibodies which could harm subsequent Rh-positive babies.

If anti-D were not given, serious complications would arise – babies could be born with severe, life-threatening anaemia, liver damage, hearing loss or learning disability. They could also suffer seizures, cardiac failure and even death.

Environmental hazards

On 26 April 1986, there was a huge explosion at the nuclear power plant at Chernobyl in the Ukraine. While it is reported that there were only 59 direct deaths, it is estimated that 7 million people, many of them living in nearby Belarus, have been exposed to unacceptably high levels of radiation as a result of the accident. To this day, there is a 27-kilometre exclusion zone around the plant. Birth defects and various childhood cancers, especially thyroid cancer, have increased dramatically in the years since the disaster in the Ukraine and neighbouring countries. It is estimated that it will take over 200 years for radiation in the exclusion zone to reach safe levels. Today, there are a total of 436 nuclear reactors in 30 different countries worldwide. Twenty-four per cent of these are in the US, but France, Germany, Japan, Korea and Russia also have substantial numbers (World Nuclear Association 2009). The UK currently has a total of 19 nuclear reactors. In Ireland, there are concerns about the Sellafield plant in Cumbria in particular. Concerns centre on its safety record and also the dumping of nuclear reactive waste from the plant into the Irish Sea.

X-ray radiation can also affect the developing embryo or foetus, especially in the first trimester. Potential effects include learning disability and leukaemia.

Other environmental pollutants include carbon dioxide, e.g. exhaust fumes in traffic-clogged cities, lead, e.g. from water pipes or lead-based paints (now banned), mercury, e.g. from polluted fish or in dental fillings, and exposure to certain fertilisers and pesticides. All of these can affect mental development in the foetus.

Maternal diseases and infections

Certain maternal diseases and infections can cause defects and complications in the newborn, either because they pass across the placenta to the foetus during pregnancy or are transmitted to the baby during the birthing process.

- **Rubella (German measles)**, while a mild disease in itself, causes serious birth defects, especially if the mother contracts it during the first trimester of pregnancy. Rubella causes prenatal and neonatal (just after birth) death, deafness, blindness, learning difficulties and heart defects. In Ireland in the past, many pregnant women contracted rubella and had babies who either died or were severely affected by the condition. Since 1971, the rubella vaccine has been administered to pre-pubertal girls, and to both boys and girls since 1988. Currently, the MMR (measles, mumps and rubella) vaccine is offered at 12 months with a booster at four to five years to all babies born in Ireland. Unfortunately, in part as a result of a much-criticised paper linking the MMR vaccine and autism, vaccine uptake for MMR dropped to 80 per cent, thus putting the population again at risk of rubella (Deer 2009). Women who are thinking of becoming pregnant should have a blood test to confirm their immunity to the disease.

- **Diabetes** occurring in non-diabetic women during pregnancy is called gestational diabetes. It occurs in approximately 4 per cent of pregnancies, but women who are obese are much more likely to develop it. Usually if women monitor their diet and take regular exercise, gestational diabetes does not pose problems. Sometimes, however, pre-eclampsia occurs, where the mother's blood pressure rises to unacceptable levels and protein appears in the urine. Babies of women who have badly controlled diabetes mellitus type 1 and 2 (meaning they have diabetes even when not pregnant) are at an increased risk of birth defects and prematurity.

- **Pre-eclampsia**, which can also occur in women with no gestational diabetes, can affect up to 10 per cent of pregnancies. It is most common in women who have had it in previous pregnancies, older women, obese women and women carrying twins or more. If blood pressure gets unacceptably high, the baby will be delivered early either by induction or Caesarean section, as failure to do so could cause serious brain damage.

HIV and AIDS

AIDS is a life-threatening infection (usually sexually transmitted) caused by the human immunodeficiency virus (HIV). A mother can infect her offspring with HIV in a number of different ways: during pregnancy across the placenta, during birth through contact with maternal blood or fluids, or through breastfeeding. However, transmission rates from mother to baby can be reduced to approximately 2 per cent if anti-viral drugs are given during pregnancy, the baby is delivered by Caesarean section and is not breastfed. If babies are born HIV positive, their average life expectancy is very low (three years) in countries where they are left untreated. Life expectancy improves with treatment – there are some HIV-positive babies still alive who are now in their teens.

Since the introduction of the antenatal HIV screening programme in Ireland in 1999, mother-to-child transmission of HIV has been dramatically reduced. Of the total of 106 babies born to HIV-infected mothers in 2008, only two were diagnosed with HIV infection, and one of these was born to a mother who was not known to be infected during pregnancy and who later tested positive.

Genital herpes

Genital herpes simplex is an incurable sexually transmitted infection caused by the herpes simplex virus (HSV). There are two distinct types of HSV. Type 2 is most commonly associated with genital infection. Type 1 has also been found to cause genital infection but is more commonly associated with oral herpes (cold sores). Most infected individuals experience no symptoms or mild symptoms. If present, symptoms include one or more blisters at the site of infection and a burning sensation during urination. After the initial infection, HSV remains dormant in the body for life and may reactivate from time to time. In 2006, 455 cases of genital herpes simplex were notified to the National Health Protection Surveillance Centre by clinics and GPs. However, it is likely that the true numbers are higher, as some people do not show symptoms and therefore go undiagnosed. If a baby passes through the birth canal of a woman with an active case of genital herpes, then the risk to the baby is high – they may die or suffer brain damage. Therefore, a Caesarean is normally performed in these cases.

Syphilis

Syphilis is a serious sexually transmitted infection caused by the bacterium *Treponema pallidum*. If it goes untreated, it can have serious effects on all the organs of the body. Unlike rubella, which damages organs during organogenesis, syphilis attacks organs after they have formed, causing blindness, learning delay, seizures and even death.

Other factors

Other factors that may affect prenatal development are maternal age, maternal diet and maternal stress, as well as paternal factors. Each of these will now be looked at briefly in turn.

Maternal age

When considering maternal age and foetal development, two age groups are significant – adolescence and women aged over 35.

According to figures from the Crisis Pregnancy Agency, the Irish teenage birth rate has remained fairly constant over the past 30 years, with approximately 2,500 teenagers giving birth annually (Crisis Pregnancy Agency 2005). Pregnant adolescents younger than 17 years have a higher incidence of medical complications involving mother and child than do adult women, although these risks are greatest for the youngest teenagers. The incidence of having a low birth weight infant (weighing less than 2,500 grams) among adolescents is more than double the rate for adults, and the neonatal death rate (within 28 days of birth) is almost three times higher. The mortality rate for the mother, although low, is twice that for adult pregnant women. Why is this? Several factors are believed to be involved:

- Immature reproductive system.
- Low pre-pregnancy weight and height.
- Poor nutrition.
- Low socio-economic status resulting in poverty.
- Low education levels.
- High rates of sexually transmitted infections.
- Substance misuse – cigarettes, alcohol and other drugs.
- Inadequate prenatal care.

When women reach age 35 and older, the risk of low birth weight, preterm delivery and foetal death also increases, as well as the risk of having a baby with Down's syndrome.

Maternal diet

A balanced diet is essential during pregnancy for the baby's general health. Obese women can pose a risk to their developing baby – there is an increased risk of prenatal death, gestational diabetes and pre-eclampsia (see above). Recent studies of children whose mothers gained excessive weight during pregnancy have shown that they are more prone to childhood and adolescent obesity themselves. Folic acid is also important, as mentioned earlier, for the prevention of neural tube defects and should be taken in tablet form to supplement dietary sources such as orange juice.

Maternal stress

When a pregnant woman experiences intense stress, there is an increase in the stress hormone cortisol, both in her blood and the amniotic fluid surrounding her unborn baby. Cortisol has been found to pass from amniotic fluid to babies of highly stressed women. The main cause of stress in pregnant women is relationship problems. While some studies (Glover et al. 2005) link stress during pregnancy with premature delivery, lower IQ and anxiety and attention problems in children, others believe that these effects merely reflect the environment the baby is born into or the effects of stressed mothers using alcohol or other drugs to cope with the stress.

Paternal factors

There are a number of paternal factors that are thought to adversely affect foetal development.

- Exposure to radiation, lead, mercury, cocaine and certain pesticides can cause sperm abnormalities leading to increased rates of miscarriage and childhood cancer.
- Men whose diet is low in vitamin C also have increased rates of birth defects and cancer.
- Fathers who smoke during and after their partner's pregnancy may have children of low birth weight. Later, if the father continues to smoke, babies are at an increased risk of cot death and childhood cancers.
- Fathers of advanced age (40+) are also more likely to have children with birth defects, although the link is much stronger between birth defects and maternal age.

Prenatal care

Prenatal care in Ireland normally takes the form of a schedule of medical visits with an obstetrician, one or more scans and a series of free prenatal classes that provide useful information on all aspects of pregnancy and birth. There are other options available, such as midwife-led units in Drogheda and Cavan, where women without risk factors for pregnancy and labour can attend throughout their pregnancy and be cared for by experienced midwives and their GP, giving birth in a homely environment. Home births and water births are also becoming increasingly popular.

The type of education provided in prenatal care varies depending on the stage of pregnancy the woman is at. In early pregnancy, topics will include information on dangers to the foetus, foetal development, common discomforts during pregnancy, factors that increase the risk of preterm labour, symptoms of preterm labour, nutrition, rest and exercise. Later prenatal classes normally focus on the birth, infant care and feeding and women's own postpartum care.

Good prenatal care involves taking regular exercise. Many women become inactive during pregnancy, believing that it could bring on premature labour. The opposite is actually the case – women who take regular moderate exercise three or four times a week actually have a reduced risk of preterm delivery and low birth weight babies than women who exercise intensively every day or women who take little or no exercise during pregnancy (Campbell and Mottola 2001).

Women from lower socio-economic groups, younger women and women who feel negatively about being pregnant are less likely to attend prenatal classes. This can have a negative effect on both mother and baby.

Birth

The birth process occurs in three stages.

- **Stage one:** This stage begins with the mother having uterine contractions and usually the amniotic sac rupturing (waters breaking). Initially, contractions will be 15 to 20 minutes apart, increasing toward the end of this stage to every three to five minutes. During this stage, the cervix (opening to the womb) dilates to approximately 10 centimetres (4 inches) in order to allow the baby's head to pass into the birth canal. This is the longest stage of the birthing process, lasting 12 to 14 hours on average for a first birth (it may be shorter on subsequent births). Pain relief may be offered in the form of Entonox (gas and air) or an epidural, which is an anaesthetic injected into the spine, numbing the body from the waist down. There are other alternative forms of pain relief, e.g. a TENS unit, which is a machine that emits electrical impulses to four pads on the mother's back during contractions, stimulating the release of the mother's own natural pain-relieving endorphins. The unit is controlled by the mother.
- **Stage two:** This stage begins when the baby's head begins to move down the birth canal and finishes when the baby has come out completely. During this time, contractions are almost constant and the mother must bear down hard to push the baby out of her body. This stage normally lasts between 45 minutes and an hour. Sometimes an episiotomy (surgical incision) will be made to enlarge the vagina and assist childbirth. This will be done under local anaesthetic and is usually performed if there is a risk of second- or third-degree tearing.
- **Stage three:** During this stage, the placenta, umbilical cord and other membranes detach and are expelled from the body. This stage lasts only a few minutes.

While it is very stressful for the baby, babies are well prepared for the birthing process. With each contraction, the placenta and umbilical cord are compressed, which can reduce the amount of oxygen getting to the baby. Prolonged labour can cause **anoxia**, where the baby has insufficient oxygen; in severe cases, this can lead to brain damage. During the birthing process, however, babies secrete large quantities of the stress hormones noradrenalin and adrenalin into the bloodstream. This causes the baby's heart to beat faster and blood sugar to rise, thus sending extra food and oxygen to the brain. At birth, the baby will be covered in a waxy coating called **vernix caseosa**, which protects the baby from heat loss and also aids its passage through the birth canal. Immediately after birth, the umbilical cord is cut and the baby begins breathing on its own for the first time.

Caesarean section

A Caesarean section involves having a surgical incision made through the woman's abdomen and uterus to deliver her baby in cases where a vaginal delivery is not possible or advisable. According to figures from the ESRI, one in five babies is now born by Caesarean section in Ireland today, which represents an 81.5 per cent increase since 1991. Worries over legal action may be one of the reasons why doctors are moving towards more Caesareans – they feel that while they will not be sued for doing a Caesarean, they could be sued for not doing one.

Reasons for planned Caesarean sections include:

- The baby is in a breech (bottom first) or transverse (sideways) position.
- Foetal illness or abnormality.
- The mother's pelvis is too small to allow the baby to pass through.
- The mother has a history of multiple Caesareans.
- Infection, e.g. herpes, that may be passed on to the baby if it is delivered vaginally.

Assessing the newborn

Very shortly after birth, the newborn baby is weighed, cleaned up and assessed for any signs of developmental problems that may require urgent attention. The **Apgar scale**, which was developed by Dr Virginia Apgar in 1952, is widely used worldwide to assess infants in the first five minutes after birth. The scale measures five things – activity and muscle tone, pulse rate, grimace (response to catheter inserted into nostril), appearance (body colour) and respiratory effort. Babies are given a score of 0, 1 or 2 for each of the five measures (see table). Scores are then added up to give an overall indication of the newborn's health.

A perfect Apgar score is a 10, but a baby who rates a 7 is considered healthy. A baby whose score ranges from 0 to 3 may need resuscitation and babies with scores in the middle, from 4 to 6, may require various interventions, including extra oxygen.

Points given	0	1	2
Activity and musle tone	Limp	Some motion of extremities	Active motion
Pulse rate	Absent	Less than 100 beats per minute	More than 100 beats per minute
Grimace (response to catheter inserted in nostril)	No response	Grimace	Cough or sneeze
Appearance – skin colour	Blue or pale	Extremities blue and body pink	Pink all over
Respiration	Absent	Slow, irregular	Regular, crying

Low birth weight, preterm and small-for-date infants

Low birth weight infants weigh less than 2.5 kilograms (5 1/2 pounds) at birth. Very low birth weight infants weigh less than 1.36 kilograms (3 pounds), and extremely low birth weight infants weigh less than 900 grams (2 pounds). **Preterm infants** are infants born more than three weeks before their due date. **Small-for-date infants** weigh 10 per cent less than the average baby of the same gestational age.

Each year, approximately 3,500 babies are born in Ireland with a low birth weight. This represents approximately 5 to 6 per cent of all births. Low birth weight is associated with many risk factors – mothers aged under 17 or over 35, poor nutrition, smoking, alcohol or other drug use, women who have had previous miscarriages or abortions and maternal stress (particularly relationship stress). Research by Farrell et al. (2008) indicates that babies of parents who were unemployed are more than twice as likely to be low birth weight than babies born to higher professionals.

There has been a huge volume of research conducted on the effects of low birth weight on subsequent development. Severity and likelihood of effects relate directly to how low the birth weight was. Effects include delayed language development, increased likelihood of learning disabilities, increased respiratory infections and asthma and increased incidence of ADHD and other emotional and behavioural disorders.

There have been huge advances in neonatal special care over the past number of decades. This has resulted in much better outcomes for low birth weight babies. In addition, practices such as kangaroo care (where the baby is held wearing just a nappy against his or her parent's bare chest for several hours per day) and infant massage therapy are now being used to counteract the effects on the baby of being cared for in incubators.

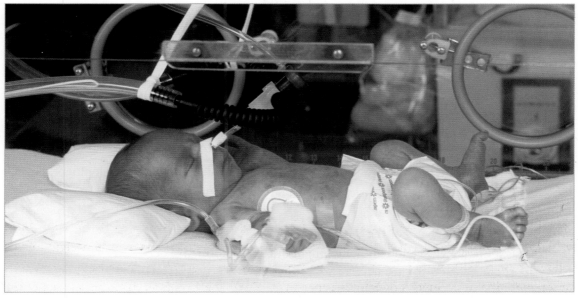

Low birth weight infant

Revision questions

1. What are genes and what is their function?
2. In genetic terms, what happens during fertilisation?
3. What is the difference between genotype and phenotype?
4. Explain the dominant-recessive gene principle.
5. Explain the sex-linked gene principle.
6. When someone is described as being a carrier of a genetically transmitted condition, what does this mean?
7. What is the most common form of Down's syndrome?
8. What are the effects of Down's syndrome on the individual?
9. Name three conditions associated with sex-linked chromosomal abnormalities.
10. What is sickle cell anaemia?
11. Describe the symptoms of cystic fibrosis.
12. Spina bifida is described as a neural tube defect. What does this mean?
13. How can a woman reduce the risk of her baby having spina bifida?
14. What is PKU and how is it diagnosed in newborns?
15. Prenatal diagnostic testing is now widely available for couples. Describe three prenatal diagnostic tests.
16. List five possible reasons for a couple experiencing infertility.

17. Describe a treatment option available for couples experiencing fertility problems.
18. Name and describe the three stages of prenatal development.
19. What is meant by the term 'organogenesis'?
20. What is a teratogen?
21. What effect can each of the following have on the unborn foetus: (a) alcohol (b) nicotine and (c) cocaine?
22. Why would a mother with Rhesus-negative blood be monitored closely during pregnancy?
23. Name four environmental hazards that can affect prenatal development.
24. Describe three maternal diseases and infections that can affect prenatal development.
25. What effect can maternal age have on prenatal development?
26. What is meant by prenatal care?
27. Describe the three stages of the birth process.
28. What is a Caesarean section and why might one be performed?
29. What is the Apgar scale and what is it used for?
30. What is meant by (a) low birth weight (b) preterm and (c) small-for-date infants?
31. What risks are associated with the above?

CHAPTER THREE

Assessment and Child Observation

Chapter outline

- Assessment (FETAC Level 6 only)
- Child observation
- Principles of good practice
- Observation methods
- Revision questions

Assessment (FETAC Level 6 only)

Definitions of assessment

Aistear defines assessment as 'the ongoing process of **collecting, documenting, reflecting on, and using** information to develop rich portraits of children as learners in order to support and enhance their future learning'. (NCCA 2009: 72)

Broadly speaking there are two types of assessment:

- Assessment **of** learning
- Assessment **for** learning

It is important for practitioners to fully understand the difference between the two types of assessment and to appreciate the purposes and uses of both.

Assessment *of* learning

This is the type of assessment that has been traditionally used by our education system. Children are given various tests and assessments; the results are arrived at and reported upon. In pre-school settings observations are carried out and findings compared to norms for the child's age group. In primary schools standardised tests such as the Drumcondra or Micra-T are used. At second level, class and end of year tests, junior and leaving certificate examinations are used. These are all examples of assessment **of** learning, the purpose of which is to gather data about a child's progress and use this data to inform others about the child's achievements. Nowadays, however, this form of assessment alone is seen as insufficient and therefore should not be the only form of assessment carried out with children in any setting. Assessment **of** learning can also be called summative assessment in that a summary or report of the child's progress to date is arrived at.

Assessment *for* learning

With assessment **for** learning, assessment is **part** of the learning process, rather than something that happens at the end of the learning process and tests what has been learned. Assessment **for** learning can also be called formative assessment, where the intention is to form, shape or guide the **next step** in learning. Assessment for learning, often abbreviated to AFL, is always **forward looking**. With AFL the practitioner always shares the **learning intention** (learning goal or goals) with the learner. They then help the child to unpack the learning intention, assisting them to understand exactly what it is they are being challenged to learn or do. As the child progresses through the learning experience the adult gives the child focused feedback and guidance where necessary. This feedback gives the child a clear picture of what they are doing well and helps them plan for how they can further progress their learning. This may seem like a lofty idea – how do you share a learning intention with a four-year-old?

Example

It is coming up to St Patrick's day and you want to help children with their scissor skills. You show the children some paper shamrocks; some have been cut out well and some have been cut out (deliberately) badly. Examine both types of shamrock and discuss with the children why they think some shamrocks turned out well and others not so well. Demonstrate how to hold the scissors and the paper. Have the children practise on other pieces of paper marked with lines and

curves, before they try the shamrocks. Allow the children themselves to decide when they are ready to start their shamrocks; do not hurry them. As the children begin working, assist and guide where necessary. Tell children that they can try as many shamrocks as they like.

What is assessed?

Assessment enables the adult to gain a lot of valuable information about children and their learning. They gain information about:

1. **Children's dispositions** or personality characteristics impact on their learning and include skills such as concentration and perseverance, curiosity and willingness to try new things, positivity, resilience and tolerance.

2. **Children's skills** in all areas of development include:
   - Physical skills such as walking, climbing, cutting, writing etc.
   - Intellectual skills such as memory, problem solving and concept formation.
   - Language skills such as listening, understanding, speaking, reading and writing.
   - Emotional skills such as emotional regulation, emotional security, self esteem and self concept.
   - Social skills such as interacting effectively with others, moral development and understanding social norms.

3. **Children's knowledge and understanding** of the key aspects of the curriculum, e.g. Aistear or primary school curriculum.

4. **Developmental milestones:** Children's development is uneven (e.g. a child may have very advanced language skills compared to their physical skills) and does not happen at the same rate for each child. However, developmental milestones can be useful for Early Childhood Care and Education (ECCE) practitioners, who may notice early signs of potential difficulties and can bring their concerns to parents and help them contact health and other educational professionals.

Purpose of assessment

There are **nine** main reasons why assessments are carried out in ECCE settings (some of these reasons apply also to child observation – see below):

1. To understand where individual children are in terms of their physical, intellectual (cognitive), language, social and emotional development, so that experiences planned are developmentally appropriate, yet challenging for them as individuals.

2. To evaluate how well children are achieving the aims and goals of the early years curriculum (Aistear).

3. To provide parents with a record of children's learning so that they can reinforce and support this learning at home.

4. To be informed about individual children's developmental progress, which may help practitioners notice early signs of developmental delay, allowing them to bring their concerns to parents, who can then contact health and other educational professionals for more specialist diagnostic assessment.

5. To observe children exhibiting problem behaviour, to investigate frequency and possible triggers and how staff are responding to the behaviour.

6. When children are involved in their own assessments they get feedback on their learning, which motivates them and allows them to plan what they want to do next.

7. Assessment gives the reflective practitioner information on how well their work is going. Results of assessment may prompt the practitioner to plan particular activities differently, change educational or care routines, arrange areas of the setting differently or obtain different materials or more of certain materials and resources.

8. Daily diaries or records of care are kept for babies and children under three (maybe longer for children with special needs). These records are very important for parents, especially if, for example, the child is taken ill and medical staff need to know how much fluid the child had consumed or how the child's mood had been during that day.

9. The childcare regulations (2006) require that progress records are kept in relation to children in childcare – see regulation 14 (f). In addition, standard 8.6 of the national standards for pre-school services (2010) requires 'staff to observe and record as appropriate, what children do, and use their observations to plan the next steps for the children's play, learning and development'. (National Standards for Pre-school Services 2010: 15)

How can assessments be documented and stored?

Assessments can be documented in a number of ways.

- **Samples of children's work:** Children should be encouraged to create a portfolio of their work. Portfolios can take the form of a scrapbook or folder where actual pieces of work or photographs of larger pieces of work (e.g. a construction piece) are stuck in. Children should be involved in choosing which pieces go into their portfolio. Sometimes children like to bring the work they are most proud of home to display it. They should be allowed to do so, and a photograph or photocopy can be kept in their portfolio.

- **Information Communications Technology (ICT):** With parental permission, photographs, video and audio recordings can be used to document children's learning and development. Practitioners can use video recordings in particular to observe groups of children involved in activities. Sometimes during the hustle and bustle of an activity it can be difficult for practitioners to observe and evaluate learning; ICT helps with this reflective practice.

- **Daily diaries or records of care:** The practitioner (usually the child's key worker) makes notes in a communications copy regarding a child's care routines, e.g. what and how much they eat, how much they sleep and details of nappy changes. Notes on the child's daily activities can also be included together with photographs of the child on particular days. This copy is sent home with the child in the evenings.
- **Checklists:** The practitioner uses pre-prepared checklists to record particular aspects of children's learning and development, e.g. pre-writing skills.
- **Observation notes and records:** Practitioners are observing the children in their setting all the time. Observations can be recorded quickly in the form of brief notes or in more detail using various observation methods and their corresponding reports, e.g. time samples, event samples, narrative observations and pre-coded language observations.

Storage of assessment information

Assessment information may be stored in various ways.

- **Central files** containing certain types of information about children should be kept in a secure location in the setting. It is best to have an office with a lockable, fireproof filing cabinet for this purpose. Information such as parents' names and contact details, medical information or copies of reports from other professionals, e.g. physiotherapists, are usually stored in individual files and alphabetically arranged in the cabinet. It is important that, while this information is kept secure, staff working with the child have access to the information if required. In addition to physical paper-based information, settings may have information stored electronically on computer. Computers should be password protected.
- **Learning portfolios:** Each child in the setting should have an individual learning portfolio in which selected samples of their work are stored. Portfolios can take the form of a folder, scrapbook or box. Children should be involved in decisions about what goes into their learning portfolio to encourage them to think about the quality of the work they are producing and the amount of effort they are putting into it. Photographs with captions can be included, of larger pieces of work, or of activities that do not have an end product.
- **Practitioner files:** In most settings children have one key worker. Key workers should have a practitioner file for every child assigned to them. This may take the form of one big lever-arch file with coloured dividers separating each child's information. Information such as observation notes and records, attendance and records of conversations with

parents or other staff members about the child can be kept here. Information in practitioner files may be transferred to a central file at the end of the year.

Methods of assessment

Traditionally, assessment was seen as something that was very much adult-led. More recently, however, early years practitioners use and value more child-led assessment methods alongside the traditional methods. Five assessment methods are examined below:

- self-assessment (child-led)
- conversations (child-led)
- observation (adult-led) (See **Child observation** below)
- task-setting (adult-led)
- testing (adult-led)

Self-assessment

Self-assessment is a very important part of assessment **for** learning, discussed earlier in this chapter. When self-assessment goes well, children begin to be able to think about what they have done, said or made and about what they would like to do differently or better next time. This works best when children have a clear idea of what they are trying to achieve. They then have a yardstick by which to measure what they have done. Terms such as 'learning intention' and 'learning goal' are used to describe this (but not to the children).

Setting learning goals: Sometimes adults set learning goals for children; these are often called WILFs – What I'm Looking For. An example of a WILF might be, 'We are going to colour the flower as neatly as we can.'

Note: The children are given their own set of colouring pencils (not crayons, as it is impossible to colour accurately with them) and a flower to colour. Choose a flower that has a number of small sections to colour so children do not get bored. This also helps co-ordination and pencil control. This is not a particularly creative exercise – it is more an exercise designed to help fine motor skills.

Other times children set their own goals. Adults can help children clarify their learning goals by providing resources to give ideas and by asking prompting questions. This does not stilt creativity, but can give children a starting point.

Examples of resources:

- Books and magazines.
- Internet access.
- Photographs and examples of other children's work.

Examples of prompting questions:

- I wonder how we could . . .?
- What do you think would happen if . . .?
- What do we need to . . .?
- Where do you want to start?
- What are you planning to do?
- What do you want to do?
- How do you think you should start?

Once children are clear on their learning goals and work through them, their learning will benefit greatly from self-assessment. Adults can help children self-assess by again asking prompting questions:

- How did you make that?
- What did you use?
- How would it have turned out if . . .?
- Would you do anything differently next time?
- How did you think of that idea?
- What did you find easy about this work?
- What did you find most difficult about this work?
- What part of this work did you enjoy?
- Are you happy with . . .?
- What did you learn from this?
- What would help you to do this better next time?

Conversations

Conversations between adult and child or child and child are very much part of all assessment methods, with the exception, perhaps, of testing. As part of assessment, the adult uses various conversation strategies to give them a better understanding of what children can do and understand.

Examples of conversation strategies:

- **Open questions:** These questions should be used most often as they invite the child to think and elaborate on their answers. Examples of open questions: Have you any ideas? Why do you think that happened? How did you do that? What were you thinking when?
- **Closed questions:** These questions are limited in terms of the response they require from children. They ask the child for short factual answers, and while they should not be used all the time, they can be useful to get the conversation going. Examples: What colours did you use? Did you enjoy building the bricks? Which is your favourite picture?
- **Thinking out loud:** Sometimes if the adult 'thinks out loud' about a problem this can prompt children to offer their opinions and suggestions. In this way the adult can assess their understanding of particular concepts. For example, an adult is transferring water from one vessel to another using a small spoon. S/he says, 'This is going to take ages, I will have to think of a better way to do this.'
- **Expressing an opinion:** Children should be encouraged to offer an opinion and to justify it. For example, 'I think Paul was very selfish in this story; what do you think, Lara?' 'What do you think we should use to stick this together, Amy?'
- **Listening to children's conversations:** Practitioners should listen carefully to children's conversations with each other while they work. Valuable information can be gained about children's knowledge and understanding. Notes should be taken and kept in the practitioner's file.

Task-setting

As children learn by doing, task-setting is a useful way to assess children's learning. Task-setting is one of the principle tools of assessment **for** learning. Adults may set tasks such as a piece of work or a project for children when they have been focusing on a particular topic. For task-setting to be successful children need to know exactly what they are being asked to do; this ensures they have a clear idea of what is required for success.

Example

Tony has set up an obstacle course outside for the children to use. He believes that the course will be useful for encouraging gross motor skills and also social skills such as waiting patiently in turn. Tony takes a group of six pre-school children out on the course. He demonstrates how to complete each part of the course and the children copy what he does. The children then take turns completing the course on their own. Tony shows them how to time each other with a stopwatch.

Testing

Testing is not commonly used in the pre-school setting except by health or other educational professionals working with children suspected of having a special need. Commercially produced, standardised tests are used by some professionals to test particular aspects of children's development such as motor skills, social skills, language skills and behaviour. Results of tests are usually represented by comparing scores with those of children of the same age.

Most Irish children are introduced to testing for the first time in the second half of Senior Infants when literacy and numeracy screening occurs. One of the screening instruments used in Irish schools is the Drumcondra Test of Early Literacy (DTEL). This is a screening and diagnostic test suitable for use with pupils at the end of Senior Infants and the beginning of First Class who are experiencing some difficulty in learning to read. The DTEL-Screening (DTEL-S) and the DTEL-Diagnostic (DTEL-D) tests draw on international best practice in early reading assessment to provide tests suitable for the Irish context. The tests complement a teacher's observations and assessments of a child's performance and increase understanding of particular difficulties. They provide information on young children's literacy difficulties so that instruction can be improved upon. In addition, at end of First Class all children complete the Drumcondra (both literacy and mathematics), Micra-T (literacy) or Sigma-T (mathematics) tests. Results are normally presented as a STen score – (score 0–10): a score of 5 or 6 is average.

It is important to treat the results of these tests with caution as certain factors can distort results, for instance, a child doing such a test with English as his or her second or third language. Having said this, testing does alert practitioners to children who may be experiencing difficulties and this is particularly important so that early intervention measures can be put in place.

Child Observation

Child observation is an important skill that must be learned and practised by everyone working with children. Childcare workers are informally observing children all the time. This chapter focuses more on formal observations, where the observer sits down to purposefully observe one or more children, creating a written record of findings.

There are four main reasons why formal observations are carried out in childcare settings:

1. To understand where children are at in terms of their physical, intellectual (cognitive), language and emotional development so that the activities planned are developmentally appropriate yet challenging for them.
2. To have a record of children's progress for parents or other professionals as may be required.
3. To be informed about individual children's developmental progress, perhaps identifying signs of developmental delay that may require further investigation.
4. To observe children exhibiting problem behaviour to investigate frequency, possible triggers and how staff are responding to the behaviour.

Principles of good practice

There are **three** main principles of good practice when carrying out child observations: confidentiality, accurate description and objectivity.

Confidentiality

As an acknowledgement of the rights of the child and their family, any information gathered while carrying out observations must be treated with the strictest confidence. In practice, this means:

- You must ask for and get permission to carry out the observation from the child's parent or primary carer before beginning. You should explain beforehand what the observation will involve and who will have access to the information gathered. If you are a student on placement, permission should be sought from your workplace supervisor. They may then approach the child's parents; alternatively, some childcare facilities have other arrangements in place with parents. **You must have either a parent's or supervisor's signature recorded at the end of each observation to show you received permission.**
- Never record the child's name or the name of the childcare facility where the observation was carried out. Instead, use TC (target child) and describe the childcare facility in general terms, e.g. large crèche in urban setting.
- Qualified childcare workers should not discuss observations outside the workplace setting. Students, however, may have to discuss aspects of their observations with their college tutor. If this is the case, then the child's anonymity should be preserved at all times.

Accurate description

Everyday speech is full of inaccuracies and exaggerations – 'I nearly died laughing', 'I'll kill him',

'He was flying'. For child observations to be of worth, they must be as accurate as possible. This is why you should be very careful about how you record information. In particular, it should not contain your own assumptions (what you think is going on), but only what is directly observable. Study the table below, which illustrates how observations should and should not be written.

Should	Should not
TC appears to be very angry.	TC is very angry.
TC appears to be looking at the teacher.	TC is looking at the teacher.
TC is holding a red colouring pencil in her right hand. Using a mature tripod grasp, she is drawing large circles with several smaller ones inside.	TC is scribbling on a piece of paper. She can hold the pencil correctly.
TC is pushing child B with her right hand on child B's back. Child B is turning round, saying, 'Stop, TC. Teacher, tell TC to stop.' Child B pushes TC once with his right hand on TC's chest.	TC is pushing child B because he is annoying her. Child B is well fit for TC and pushes her back.

Objectivity

The Oxford Dictionary defines objectivity as a 'judgment based on observable phenomena and uninfluenced by emotions or personal prejudices'. For child observations to be accurate and worthwhile, they must be objective. As you get to know the children being observed, however, this can become more and more difficult. You must be aware of the following.

- Your previous knowledge of the child may cause you to interpret what you observe in an inaccurate way.
- Your own emotional response to the child, whether it is negative or positive, may cause you to observe in a biased fashion.
- The aim or purpose of the observation may distort your findings in that you may begin interpreting things in a biased way in order to 'find what you were looking for'.

Observers must make every effort not to allow the factors listed above to influence their observations and instead accurately record what they see and hear.

Some students ask tutors if they can carry out their observations for assessment on their own children. Tutors often advise against this on the grounds of objectivity. Can you see how a parent could have difficulty carrying out an objective observation with their own child?

Observation methods

There are a number of different ways in which observations may be recorded. The following methods will be outlined here:

- Narrative
- Pre-coded
- Checklist
- Time sample
- Event sample
- Movement or flow charts
- Tables, pie charts and bar charts
- Using audio or video recordings during observations

Narrative

With this method, the observer writes down exactly what the child is doing and saying while being observed. The child is usually observed for 10 minutes or less with this method, as it is quite difficult for the observer to record such detailed information over a more extended period. Codes are usually used to help speed up note taking (see below). Observations should be written up properly from the notes as soon as possible afterwards.

Codes

In order to speed up note taking while observing children, various coding systems may be used. One of the most commonly used is a system developed by Kathy Sylva and her colleagues (1980) as part of a preschool research project. They developed a total of 30 different codes, some of which are listed below.

Code	Meaning
TC	Target child (child being observed)
C	Other child
A	Adult (staff member, parent, student)
→	Speaks to, e.g. TC → A

Advantages

- No special equipment is needed – pen, paper, eyes and ears.
- It trains the observer to really listen to and carefully watch the children in their care.
- Because the observer writes down everything they observe, it can be a very objective method.

The observer is not setting out beforehand to observe one or more specific behaviours.

- It provides detailed information about the child.

Disadvantages

- It can be difficult to observe and note everything, especially until the observer has developed a good system of coded note taking.
- Because they are so detailed, narratives are generally carried out over a period of no more than 10 minutes. As such, this can give an atypical picture of the child being observed.
- Because the observer has to give this type of observation their full attention, it can be difficult to find uninterrupted time to carry it out.

See a sample observation carried out using the narrative method in Chapter 5, pp. 116–120.

Pre-coded

With language development observations, a pre-coded technique is often used. With this method, only what the child and those around them **says** is recorded. This makes this observation different from the narrative method described above, where everything the child does **and** says is recorded in great detail. Codes (as described above) are used to allow the observer to accurately record everything that is said. A key to the codes is often given at the beginning of the observation. With permission, conversations may be taped for coding afterwards.

Example

A→TC (adult speaks to target child)

TC→A (target child speaks to adult)

TC→C (target child speaks to another child)

Code	Language
A→TC	What did you get up to at school today?
TC→A	Huh?
A→TC	Did you get to do anything good at school today?

Advantages

- No special equipment is needed – pen, paper and ears.
- It trains the observer to listen carefully to children in their care.
- Because the observer writes down everything the child says, it is a very objective method.

- It provides detailed information about the child's language.
- Codes make it easier to accurately record information.

Disadvantages

- It can be difficult to note everything the child says, particularly if the child is older and speaks quickly.
- Pre-coded observations, because they are so detailed, are generally carried out over a period of no more than 10 minutes, which can give an atypical picture of the child being observed.
- Because the observer has to give this type of observation their full attention, it can be difficult to find uninterrupted time to carry it out.

Checklist

This type of observation uses a list of skills typical for the age group of the child you are observing. This method is most commonly used for physical and social development observations where behaviour and skills are easily seen. Suitable lists are obtained from recognised developmental guides and textbooks. The source of the checklist should always be listed on the observation.

The observer observes the child, usually over an extended period of time, and ticks off skills as they are observed. If an item is ticked off, the observer should note why they ticked the item off, i.e. what evidence they observed that made them conclude the child could master the skill. If it is observed that a child has not yet mastered a skill on the list, then an X should be put beside that item, and again, evidence should be provided for this decision. If some items on the list are not observed, this too should be recorded (N/O).

Excerpt from a checklist observation: physical development (gross motor skills), 12 months

Observation			
Directions Put a ✓ beside items you have observed and an X beside those skills which you observed TC cannot yet master. Put N/O beside items you have not had the opportunity to observe.			
Item		**Evidence**	**Date**
Can sit alone indefinitely	✓	Sits for over 10 minutes taking bricks in and out of a bucket	23/11
Can get into a sitting position from lying down	✓	Gets into a sitting position from lying down after nappy change	23/11

Can pull themselves to stand and walk around furniture (coasting)	✓	Walks around holding onto toy boxes	24/11
Can return to sitting without falling	✓	Returns to sitting after walking round toy boxes	24/11
May stand alone for short periods	✓	Stands for a few seconds after walking round toy boxes before putting hands out to crawl	23/11
Walks with one hand held	✓	Walks unsteadily with one hand held by carer for nappy changing	23/11
May walk alone with feet wide apart and arms raised for balance	✗	Does not walk alone yet	
May bottom-shuffle or bear walk	✓	Bottom shuffles over to retrieve soft toy in home corner	23/11
Crawls up stairs and comes down backwards (still unsafe)	N/0	No stairs in crèche	

Advantages

- Information is quick and easy to record. Unlike narrative, the observer does not have to be looking and listening to the child 100 per cent of the time. Observer may therefore be able to carry out other duties while the observation is being done.
- When complete, information about the child is available at a glance.
- Observations can be carried out over a number of days, making it more likely to be a true reflection of the child's stage of development.
- Compiling and using checklists makes the observer more familiar with milestones of development.

Disadvantages

- Information gathered is limited to what is required by the checklist. Therefore, relevant information may not be recorded.
- Checklists put great emphasis on the 'norms' of development and do not take account of the fact that while children follow a similar developmental pattern, they all develop in their own unique way.

See a sample observation carried out using the checklist method in Chapter 4, pp. 91–4.

Time sample

This method is used to get a general picture of a child's activities, social group and language interactions. It is sometimes used if staff are concerned that an individual child is having difficulty interacting with other children. The target child is observed at fixed time intervals, e.g. every 30 minutes over a three-hour period. For objectivity, time intervals must be decided in advance. It is a useful method in that the child does not have to be watched continuously. Observations are usually organised under preset headings such as:

- Actions (what the child is doing).
- Social group (who the child is with).
- Language (what the child is saying).

Excerpt from a time sample observation: social development, three years

Time	Actions	Social group	Language
12.30	Standing looking towards children playing in sand pit	On own	Not speaking
1.00	Playing with action figures (wrestlers) – banging them off each other as if they are fighting	On own	Wha! Wha! Wha! Take that!
1.30	Eating lunch	Group of 8 children around lunch table	Can I have the strawberry yoghurt instead of this? (mandarin yogurt)
2.00			
2.30			
3.00			
3.30			

Advantages

- It gives a good general picture of the child's activities and interactions over a period of time.
- It can be completed by staff while they carry out their normal daily routine.
- If it was suspected that a child was not interacting well with other children, it is a useful tool to obtain a more objective view of what is actually the case.

Disadvantages

- It considers only one or two areas of development – social with some language.
- Because only a sample of the child's behaviour is observed, important instances may be missed.
- The observer may forget to observe the child at the appropriate time because they were busy with other tasks.

> See a sample observation carried out using the time sample method in Chapter 7, pp. 168–72.

Event sample

'That child is always pulling toys off other kids', 'He is forever hitting the rest of them', 'She spits at the others if she doesn't get her own way'. Sometimes children are described like this because they behave in an unacceptable way in the childcare setting. However, while general statements like this may frequently be made by staff, they are not helpful and can label children unfairly. Children whose behaviour is causing concern should be observed systematically and an accurate picture of what is actually going on arrived at. Event sample is an observation method designed to do just this.

Event sample observations

- Define the behaviour that is causing concern before the observation begins.
- Record the behaviour each time it occurs.
- Record whether the behaviour was provoked or unprovoked.
- Record what happened directly before the behaviour occurred – this allows staff to investigate whether there is something triggering the behaviour. This is called the antecedent, but it may not always be known.
- Record what the consequences were for the child concerned – this can allow staff to assess how effectively they are dealing with the behaviour.

Excerpt from an event sample observation: emotional development, six years

TC is six years old and is attending an after-school programme. Since she started in the programme two months ago, she has consistently acted in a destructive way towards other children's possessions and their schoolwork.

Date	Time	Provoked or unprovoked	Antecedent	Description of behaviour	Consequence
2/11	2.50	Unprovoked	Earlier, child J was showing her new pencil case to child K.	TC hides J's new pencil case at bottom of bin in bathroom. J upset.	A asks TC to return pencil case to child J and apologise.
2/11	3.30	Unprovoked	Child L asks staff member if she thinks his picture is neat – staff member praises him for keeping within the lines.	TC scribbles on L's picture. When M reacts, TC tells L that she can scribble on her picture.	A asks TC why she has scribbled on the the picture – TC shrugs and says 'sorry L'.
3/11	3.40	Provoked	Child M loudly tells a staff member that TC was in trouble again at big school and that their teacher said 'she was sick of TC's nonsense'.	TC begins to shout loudly at M, using bad language towards her.	A tells M that she she shouldn't be carrying tales and puts TC in time out for using bad language.

Advantages

- Behaviour that is causing concern can be investigated in a fair and systematic way.
- It may shed light on what is triggering the behaviour.
- It can help staff evaluate how effectively they are dealing with the problematic behaviour.

Disadvantages

- The child may begin to realise that his or her behaviour is being monitored and recorded, which can have the effect of making the situation worse.
- No account is taken of external factors that may be influencing the child's behaviour, e.g. family problems.
- Only negative problematic behaviours are recorded.

Movement or flow charts

As the name suggests, movement or flow charts record a child's movements within the childcare setting over a specified period of time. They are generally used to track or monitor a child's use of equipment and resources. When complete, flow charts show at a glance how a child spent his or her day. Sometimes a number of flow charts are carried out with different children to discover what toys and activities are most and least preferred. It can also be used to observe children's concentration levels. Sometimes the findings of the flow chart are summarised (see below).

Excerpt from a flow chart sample observation (three years)

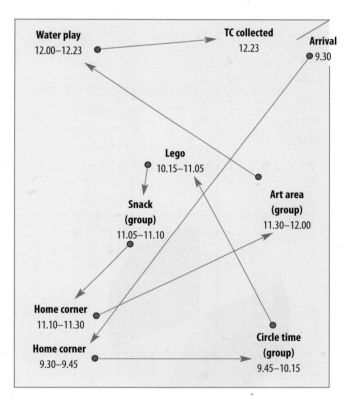

Advantages

- It is a quick method that can be carried out while the staff member is carrying on with daily duties.
- It is a useful method for showing the play preferences of one or more children (if a number of flow charts are created).
- It can clearly show which pieces of play equipment and activities are favoured by the children.
- It can indicate a child's concentration levels.

Disadvantages

- It does not give any detail, e.g. you may know from a flow chart that a child spent 30 minutes in the sand and water area, but you will know nothing of what he or she did there. However, it can be used in combination with other methods, which would solve this problem.
- If a child is very active, the flow chart may become confusing and difficult to interpret. A summary of findings should therefore be written (as above) soon after the flow chart is completed.

Tables, pie charts and bar charts

Strictly speaking, tables, pie charts and bar charts are not observation methods, but rather methods of representing information gathered about children in the workplace. They can be used to display information about virtually anything, but in the childcare setting they are usually used to display information about equipment usage.

Child	Home corner	Sand	Water	Small world toys	Book area
Mark			✓	✓	
Megan	✓				✓
Laura	✓				✓
Susan	✓				
Luke		✓	✓	✓	✓
Anna					
Liam	✓	✓	✓	✓	
Mia	✓				

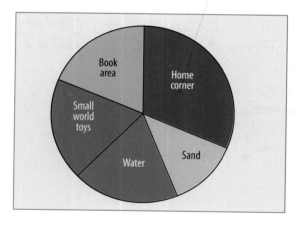

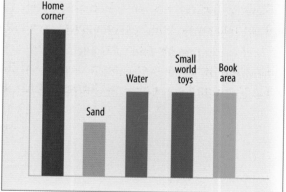

Using audio or video recordings during observations

It is advised that no video recording be carried out by students while doing observations. The reason for this is that the anonymity of the child cannot be preserved, as they can be seen on video tape. Audio tapes, on the other hand, can be used and are a useful way of recording language, especially when children get older and speak so quickly that it would be impossible to write down everything they say there and then. If you do decide to use an audio tape (tape recorder), there are some points that you must consider.

- Permission should be sought from parents before recording the speech of any child.
- The child has the right to know that they are being recorded. Discuss it with them beforehand, answering any questions, e.g. why are you recording me?
- Proper transcription of taped conversation takes considerable time – make sure you allow for this.

Revision questions

(Questions 1–7: FETAC Level 6 only)

1. Describe what is meant by 'assessment **of** learning'.
2. Describe what is meant by 'assessment **for** learning'.
3. What information does assessment give adults about children in their care?
4. What are the nine purposes of assessment?
5. Describe how assessments can be documented and stored.
6. How can children self-assess?
7. Describe four conversation strategies that adults can employ to stimulate children's conversations.

8. Give four reasons why child observations are carried out in childcare settings.
9. In relation to child observations, (a) what is confidentiality? (b) why is it important? and (c) how can childcare workers protect children's confidentiality?
10. What is meant by the term 'objectivity' in relation to child observations?
11. Name and describe four different observation methods.

CHAPTER FOUR

Physical Growth and Development

Chapter outline

- Patterns of growth
- Motor development
- Motor skills
- Promoting gross and fine motor skills (zero to six years)
- Promoting gross and fine motor skills (six to 12 years) (FETAC Level 6 only)
- Sensory and perceptual development
- Observing and recording children's physical growth and development
- How Aistear promotes physical development
- Sample observation
- Revision questions

Patterns of growth

Growth in infancy

According to figures from the Central Statistics Office, the average Irish baby now weighs in at 3.5 kilograms (7 pounds 11 ounces), with boys weighing on average 140 grams (5 ounces) more at birth than girls. In addition, the average length at birth is 51 centimetres (20 inches). After an initial weight loss after birth, usually approximately 150 grams (5 ounces), babies gain up to 150 grams (5 ounces) per week for the first month once they begin feeding well. Babies will normally have doubled their birth weight by four months and tripled it by one year. In addition, their height will also increase rapidly, with the average baby reaching 71–74 centimetres (28–29 inches) in height by their first birthday.

During the second year, growth slows considerably. By their second birthday, the average infant weighs 12.7 kilograms (2 stone) and between 81 and 89 centimetres (32 to 35 inches) in height, reaching almost half their adult height. In fact, by doubling a child's height at age two, a rough estimate of their final adult height can be obtained.

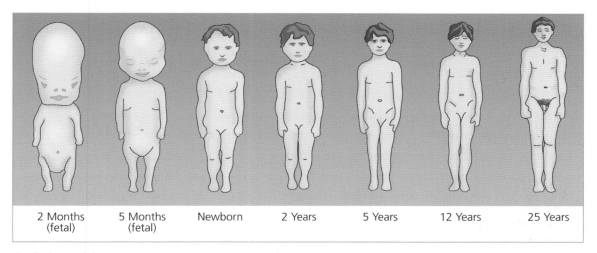

| 2 Months (fetal) | 5 Months (fetal) | Newborn | 2 Years | 5 Years | 12 Years | 25 Years |

Cephalocaudal pattern

The **cephalocaudal pattern** is the sequence of growth whereby the fastest growth always occurs at the top of the body, i.e. the head, gradually moving downwards. As a proportion of total body length at birth, a baby's head makes up one-quarter. In contrast, the head makes up only one-eighth of an adult's total body length.

Growth in early childhood (two to six years)

During the preschool and early school years, the rate of growth slows with each additional year. The head-to-body ratio evens out more as the child's trunk and limbs begin to lengthen. Children also being to lose fatty tissue and gain more lean muscle tissue (on average, boys gain more muscle tissue than girls). Up until about the age of two, most children are about the same height. As children progress towards their fourth, fifth

Children of the same age – very different heights

and sixth birthdays, however, some children will become noticeably taller or shorter than others. These differences are normally a result of heredity but may also reflect nutritional status, chronic illness or in a small number of cases, congenital problems, e.g. pituitary dwarfism.

Growth in middle and late childhood (six to 12 years) (FETAC Level 6 only)

During middle and late childhood there is a slow, steady pattern of growth. The average child grows approximately 2.5 to 5 cm per year (2–3 inches). On average, by age eight white European boys and girls are approximately 127 cm tall (4 ft 2 in) and weigh approximately 25 to 28 kg (4–4½ stone) – although see section on childhood obesity below. While the skeleton and body organs increase in size and weight, most children lose any 'baby fat' they may have had in their earlier years. As a result some children of seven to eight years of age do not weigh much more than they did two or three years earlier. Muscle tone improves, so children become much more co-ordinated and their movements more fluid. Body strength increases for both boys and girls, but because boys have proportionately more muscle cells than girls they are generally physically stronger from this age onwards. Bone density increases considerably during these years, requiring a calcium-rich diet to support this growth. Body proportions change significantly during this period; the head and waist circumference decrease in relation to overall body size.

Environmental factors – effects of family, society and culture on physical growth

Physical growth is affected by a number of different cultural and environmental factors:

Ethnic origin

Average height is increasingly used as a measure of the health and wellness (standard of living and quality of life) of populations. Studies have been conducted in countries with diverse ethnic populations such as the USA and England regarding differences in birth weight and growth patterns in childhood among different ethnic groups. These studies have consistently found that babies and children from ethnic minority groups tend to have lower average birth weights and heights than majority ethnic populations. In a 2012 study, Stunted Growth in Pre-school Children, the World Health Organisation (2012) sampled 148 developed and developing nations. This study estimated that 171 million children worldwide have stunted growth with 167 million of these living in developing countries. As an example, the study found that in Guatemala, 82 per cent of children under the age of five were judged to have stunted growth. On the other side of the coin the world's three tallest nations are the Netherlands, Denmark and Norway with the average man standing at 185 cm (6 ft 1 in) tall and the average woman 168 cm (5 ft 6 in). The three smallest nations are Bolivia (men 160 cm [5 ft 3 in], women 142 cm [4 ft 8 in]), the Philippines (men 161 cm [5 ft 3½ in], women 150 cm [4 ft 11½ in]) and India (men 165 cm [5 ft 5 in], women 152 cm [5 ft]). Genetics can partly explain these differences (the people of some nations are naturally smaller than those of others) but economic and social prosperity must also be considered.

Nutrition

Malnutrition is associated with the following issues:

- Too little of certain foods, e.g. fruit and vegetables.
- Too much of certain foods, e.g. fatty or sugary foods.
- Too little food.

These aspects of malnutrition affect how a child grows and develops. All three of these issues occur and are affecting children in Ireland on a daily basis.

Too little food: A recent study conducted by the Department of Health, The Irish Health Behaviour in School-aged Children (HBSC) Study (2010), found that 21 per cent of children aged 10 to 17 were either going to school without breakfast or going to bed without a proper meal. There are many reasons for this: sometimes children refuse breakfast (unfortunately this usually results in their filling up with high-calorie snacks mid-morning); poverty can mean there is little money for food; problems such as parental addiction or illness can mean that daily routines such as preparing and cooking meals are neglected.

Too little of certain foods and too much of others: These two factors cause many of the health problems of children in Ireland today. Growing Up in Ireland (GUI), a large longitudinal study conducted with 11,000 nine-month-olds and 8,500 nine-year-olds, launched in 2007 by the Irish Government, gives very good insights into the eating habits of Irish children today. GUI has produced a number of reports relating to various aspects of children's lives. Report 2, *Overweight and Obesity in 9 Year Olds*, concerns us here. The report (citing Perry et al. 2009) explains that between 1948 and 2002 the height of Irish 14-year-old boys increased by 16 per cent while their weight increased by 65 per cent. This finding indicates that while we are getting taller (probably because of relative economic prosperity) we are also getting much heavier.

GUI found that 22 per cent of Irish boys and 30 per cent of Irish girls were overweight or obese at nine years of age. The situation in Ireland is worse than in some other European countries and better than in others. Italy, Spain, Greece, England and Cyprus have higher obesity levels than Ireland, whereas France, Sweden, Czech Republic, Germany, Denmark and the Netherlands (with 12 per cent) have lower.

GUI also found a strong correlation between obesity levels and social class, particularly for girls. Children coming from households with professional parents have an 18 per cent (boys) or 19 per cent (girls) chance of being overweight or obese. Among the children of unskilled parents these percentages rise to 29 per cent for boys and 38 per cent for girls.

Being overweight or obese is sometimes considered to be purely physical and health-related, but it impacts on all aspects of a child's development. This issue will therefore be discussed in following chapters.

Non-organic failure to thrive

'Non-organic failure to thrive' is a term used to describe a child who is not growing or gaining weight, but for no physiological reason. Public health professionals often seem to be obsessed with children's progress in terms of weight and height. This is not without good reason. Height and appropriate weight gain indicate good health and emotional stability. Children who are neglected or abused (physically, emotionally or sexually) often show a non-organic failure to thrive. Despite eating normally they do not make sufficient progress with weight or height. Children in high-stress situations, for example those who witness domestic violence, may not sleep properly and expend huge amounts of emotional energy. This causes non-organic failure to thrive.

Chronic infections

Physical growth and development can sometimes be impaired by chronic infections. Children who regularly experience infections – usually ear, nose and throat or chest infections – often remain smaller and thinner than average. Children may be prescribed antibiotics as many as eight to 10 times per year, which depletes their immune system. They may have frequent high temperatures and be off their food for considerable periods. Also the body needs to repair itself after an infection, and nutrients such as protein, vitamins and minerals go into this process rather than towards growth. Ear, nose and throat infections are often treated by inserting ear grommets or removing tonsils and adenoids. Lung infections are not so easy to deal with – the lungs obviously cannot be removed. Excellent nutrition combined with fresh air and exercise as appropriate are therefore recommended. Breast-feeding babies has been shown to reduce the incidence of chronic infections in children.

Onset of puberty (FETAC Level 6 only)

There are wide variations in the ages at which children being to progress into puberty. For girls it may begin as early as nine or as late as 15. The age range for boys tends to be narrower, usually 11 to 13½. Children are entering puberty at younger and younger ages. One study conducted in Norway as far back as 1979 found that the age at which girls entered puberty reduced from 17 years in the 1840s to 13 years in the 1970s. The principal reason for this is improved nutrition: puberty occurs earlier in countries where children are well-fed. In the western world puberty does not generally occur until the child has reached a weight of 45 kg (7 stone). This has led to the phenomenon of some overweight children (particularly girls) entering puberty at a very early age.

Patterns of puberty for both boys and girls are usually quite set and predictable.

Girls: breasts enlarge, pubic hair appears, later hair in armpits, height increases, hips become wider than shoulders and lastly menarche appears (periods). Cycles in the beginning are often irregular. Many girls do not ovulate regularly for two years after the onset of menarche.

Boys: Increase in penis and testicle size, appearance of straight pubic hair, minor voice changes, first ejaculation, appearance of curled pubic hair, body growth, growth of armpit hair, breaking voice and lastly growth of facial hair.

All of these changes are caused by the secretion of a series of hormones by endocrine glands, namely the pituitary and hypothalamus (in the brain) and the gonads, i.e. testes and ovaries. The principal hormones secreted are testosterone in males and oestrogen in females. Onset of puberty has emotional and behavioural as well as physical implications for young people, and will be referred to again in later chapters.

Development of the brain

In the past, scientists believed that the brain's cells essentially stopped dividing early in childhood, and that therefore the child remained with whatever they were genetically born with. Since then, scientists have revised this idea, believing that the brain has **plasticity**, meaning it can adapt to changes in the child's environment.

Structure of the brain

The human brain consists of two halves, or hemispheres (often called the right and left brain). The **cerebral cortex** is the name given to the outer layer of the brain (much as the flesh of a peach covers its inner stone). Each hemisphere within the cortex consists of four lobes, or areas, each of which carries out quite specific although sometimes shared functions (see diagram). In addition, the inner core of the brain (much like the stone of a peach) contains the pituitary gland, amygdala (responsible for emotions) and the hippocampus (responsible for memory and emotions).

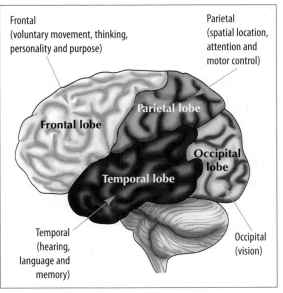

The brain's four lobes

Neurons

Neurons (nerve cells) are the basic working unit of the nervous system. Sensory neurons process information from the environment and motor neurons act on it. Within the brain, there are specialised clusters of neurons called **neural circuits** that process specific types of information. For example, there are extensive neural circuits for language and creative thinking in the left side of the brain, whereas neural circuits for logic and mathematical thinking are more extensive in the right side. In the past, this has been used to label certain people (particularly girls) as left brain dominant or others (particularly boys) as right brain dominant. Nowadays, however, this distinction is not believed to be as clear cut. Studies using brain imaging techniques now believe most brain functions involve both hemispheres.

Brain development

The brain develops most during the prenatal stage and first two years of life (the human brain reaches 75 per cent of its adult weight by two years). This is why damage experienced at either of these stages can have serious consequences. In addition, studies have shown that children living in deprived environments show considerably less brain activity than children living in more enriching environments. These effects are not irreversible, however, and children's brains are believed to be highly adaptable and resilient. Thus, if the circumstances of babies born into deprived environments change for the better, e.g. through positive interventions at home or through foster care, they can make up for lost ground and develop towards their true potential. The rule of thumb is that the sooner this happens, the better, because the brain becomes less adaptable as the child gets older.

Brain development basically means three things:

- **Myelination**, or development of the myelin sheath (an insulating layer) around neurons. This has the effect of speeding up the transmission of messages by neurons. Myelination of some neurons will occur before others, e.g. myelination of neurons connected with vision is almost complete by six months, hence infant vision is almost as clear as an adult's by six months, whereas myelination of neurons in parts of the brain connected with the development of hand–eye co-ordination is not complete until four years. Hence, children's hand–eye co-ordination is usually clumsy until then.
- **Increased connections between neurons** also result in the brain becoming more developed and sophisticated. The actual size of the brain does not increase dramatically after age two, but its internal structure, or 'wiring', does.
- **Increased specialisation of areas of the brain.**

Motor development

How does motor development occur?

There are two conflicting views about how motor development occurs. Each view reflects one side of the nature vs. nurture debate outlined in Chapter 1. Through years of detailed child observation, developmental psychologist Arnold Gesell (1934), who was very much influenced by Charles Darwin, found that babies and children develop motor skills in a fixed order and within quite specific timeframes. From this, he concluded that children's motor development follows a fixed, genetically determined plan. Gesell's work has been taken on board by many health professionals around the world. Developmental check-ups often focus on how close a child is to the **developmental norm** or average for his or her age group. Children whose pattern of development is outside the developmental norms for their age are often given further attention.

Gesell was one of the first psychologists to adopt a scientific approach to the study of child development. He used the latest technology in his 'photographic dome' to observe children without their being consciously aware that they were being observed.

In contrast to this, those who believe in the **dynamic systems theory**, such as Ester Thelen (2000), consider that motor development occurs as a result of babies acting on their environment and fine tuning their movements according to the outcomes of their actions. For babies to act on their environment, it is important that they are motivated to do so. This is why a rich environment is important not only for cognitive skills (discussed in Chapter 5), but motor skills as well. Babies who are strapped into chairs and buggies for long periods of time

Gesell's Photographic Dome – cameras rode on metal tracks at the top of the dome and were moved as needed to record the child's activities. However, did Gesell ever consider what it was like for a child to be inside the dome?

or are not given stimulating activities to do with their hands will not be motivated to develop their motor skills.

Thelen would therefore advocate that babies be left without nappies as much as possible, given toys to reach for and soft surfaces to crawl and roll around on. Toddlers should be given push-pull toys, tricycles and other equipment to develop their gross motor skills. They should also be given plenty of opportunities to develop fine motor skills, e.g. colouring, cutting and pasting, threading and beading, cookery.

Reflexes

When babies are born, they have a number of inbuilt reflexes. Reflexes are automatic responses to stimuli in the environment and do not involve the brain, only the spinal cord, and are therefore not under the infant's conscious control. Most (although not all) reflexes seem to have a survival function, which is why it is believed they are genetically programmed. Reflexes allow the newborn baby to react to their environment before they have had an opportunity to learn anything.

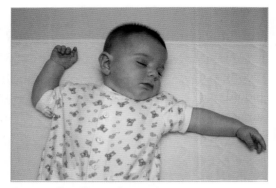

Tonic reflex (fencer's pose)

Reflex	Description	Disappears
Blinking	Baby will close both eyes in response to a flash of light or puff of air.	Permanent
Rooting	Turns head, opens mouth and begins sucking if cheek is stroked.	3–4 months
Sucking	Sucks automatically if object is placed in the mouth.	3–4 months
Grasping	Grasps finger tightly if palm is stroked.	3–4 months
Babinski	Fans out toes and turns foot in if sole is stroked.	3–4 months
Stepping	Stepping action if feet are placed on a flat surface.	3–4 months
Swimming	If infant is put face down in water, will make co-ordinated 'swimming' actions.	6–7 months
Tonic	Sometimes called fencer's pose (see photo). If baby is placed on their back, they will make a fist with both hands, turning head to the right.	2 months
Moro or startle	Responds to a sudden loud noise or movement – baby will arch its back, throw back its head and fling out its arms and legs, rapidly bringing them in towards the body again.	3–4 months

Evolutionary psychologists see the existence of these primitive reflexes as evidence of our past, when humans were covered with long body hair and climbed trees in order to escape predators. For example, the grasping reflex may have been used by babies to cling to their mother's hair, the rooting reflex so that they could locate the mother's nipple, the startle reflex to break their fall should they be dropped by their mothers and the tonic reflex to prevent the baby rolling off a surface. Some others are not as easy to explain, e.g. the stepping or Babinski reflexes.

As stated earlier, reflexes do not involve the brain. Therefore, they disappear as the brain becomes more sophisticated and takes over. If reflexes persist, this can be an indication that the brain is not developing normally.

Motor skills

Development of gross and fine motor skills (zero to six years)

The first **gross motor skills** to develop involve the large muscles of the body, such as crawling, walking, running and dancing. Later gross motor skills to develop enable, in varying degrees, more specific and highly desirable skills such as playing football and other sports. Many educationists undervalue gross motor skills. This is strange considering the importance society puts on gross motor skills and how well many of our sports people are paid for their skills.

Both gross and fine motor skills are often described in terms of when they are normally achieved. These are called **developmental milestones or norms**. While there are individual differences between children, most children achieve these milestones around the same time. The major milestones for physical development are outlined in the table below and may be used both to create developmental checklists and to evaluate observations of physical development.

Key terminology:
- **Asymmetrical movement:** Jerky, unco-ordinated movements.
- **Head lag:** The head has little control, falls back when pulled to sit.
- **Neonate:** Newborn.
- **Prone:** Lying face down.
- **Reflex:** Involuntary response to a stimulus.
- **Supine:** Lying on the back (think of S for sky – baby is facing the sky).
- **Symmetrical movement:** Balanced movement on both sides of body.
- **Ventral suspension:** Held in the air, face down.

Age	Gross motor skills	Fine motor skills
Neonate	**Reflexes present (see above)** **Prone** • Complete flexion (curled up with legs and arms bent in under body). • Lies with head to one side, resting on one cheek. • Fists clenched. **Supine** • Lies with head to one side • Knees bent in towards the body with soles of feet touching. • Random, jerky, asymmetrical kicking movements. **Ventral suspension** • Head and legs fall below the level of the back – baby makes a complete downward curve. **Sitting** • Complete head lag, back curved.	• Fists clenched. • Can focus 15–25 cm, stares at bright lights, e.g. a window. • Concentrates on carer's face when feeding.
1 month	**Reflexes present (see above)** **Prone** • Lies with head to one side but can now lift its head to change position. • Legs are no longer bent or tucked under the body. • Arms are bent away from the body, fists still usually closed. **Supine** • Head will be on one side. • Arm and leg on the side the head is facing will be held out. • Legs bent with soles of feet facing each other. **Ventral suspension** • The head is on the same level as the back and the legs are coming up to the level of the back. **Sitting** • Back is a complete curve. • Head will lag backwards while being pulled to sit, head may stay steady for a brief moment before falling forward onto chest.	• Will turn head towards the light or bright objects, e.g. TV screen. • Will follow moving objects 5–10 cm from face. • Baby will stare at carer's face when being fed or spoken to. • Hands are usually closed.

Age	Gross motor skills	Fine motor skills
3 months	**Prone** • Baby can now lift head and chest, supporting itself on elbows and forearms. • Baby may bob its head in a rocking movement. • May scratch at the floor. • Bottom flat, legs straighter, more co-ordinated kicking movements. **Supine** • Head in a central position. • Smooth, more co-ordinated movements of arms and legs. • Will kick legs strongly, sometimes alternately, sometimes together. • Waves arms symmetrically before bringing them in over body. **Ventral suspension** • Head is above the level of the back with legs on same level. **Sitting** • Head comes forward with body when pulled to sit. • Head may fall forward after a short time in the sitting position. • Little or no head lag. • When held in sitting position, back should be straight except for curve at bottom lumbar region. **Standing** • Sags at the knees when held standing. • Stepping reflex should have disappeared.	• Finger play – baby has discovered its hands and will move them around, watching them in the light. • Baby will wave its arms in excitement when it sees bottle or breast. • Can hold object such as a rattle in their hand for a short time before dropping it – may hit itself on the head. Ventral suspension
6 months	**Prone** • Can lift head and chest well clear of the floor, supporting themselves with outstretched arms – hands flat on the floor. • Can roll over from front to back and (usually) from back to front. • May pull knees up in an attempt to crawl but will slide backwards. **Supine** • Will lift head to look at feet. Will kick strongly using alternate feet. • May lift up legs and grasp one foot or both, attempting to put them in mouth.	• Uses palmer grasp to grab objects of interest. • Transfers toys from hand to hand. • Puts toys and other objects in their mouth to explore them. • May lift arms in a request to be lifted.

Age	Gross motor skills	Fine motor skills
6 months	**Sitting** • Held sitting, back will be straight and head firmly erect. • May sit alone momentarily, but is likely to topple and will not put hands out to break fall. • When hands grasped, will brace shoulders and pull themselves to sit. **Standing** • Enjoys bearing weight and will bounce up and down. • May demonstrate the parachute reflex – when held in the air and whooshed downwards, will straighten and separate arms or legs and fan out toes or fingers.	Parachute reflex
9 months	**Prone** • May rock back and forwards in an attempt to crawl. • Will move backwards in the crawling position before forwards. **Supine** • Rolls from back to front with ease – may do this to get around. **Sitting** • Can sit for 15 minutes or more without support. • Can keep balance when reaching for toys nearby. • Can return to sitting position when toy is retrieved. • Puts out arms to prevent falling. • Some babies bottom shuffle – using their legs to propel them along. **Standing** • Can pull themselves to stand from kneeling position with the aid of furniture. • When supported by an adult, will step forward on alternate feet. • May begin to step around furniture (coasting). • Cannot lower themselves to the floor from a standing position and will fall heavily back on bottom. • May crawl up stairs but cannot come down safely.	• Uses inferior pincer grasp with index finger and thumb. • Cannot let go of objects, yet will voluntarily drop or bang them onto a hard surface to release them. • Grasps objects with one hand, will inspect and transfer to other. • May bang objects, e.g. wooden blocks, together in hands. • Will poke and point at small objects, e.g. a crumb on their highchair tray.
12 months	**Sitting** • Can sit alone indefinitely. • Can get into a sitting position from lying down.	• Uses mature pincer grasp and can release objects voluntarily.

Age	Gross motor skills	Fine motor skills
12 months	**Standing** • Can pull themselves to stand and walk around furniture (coasting). • Can return to sitting without falling. • May stand alone for short periods. • Walk with one hand held. • May walk alone with feet wide apart and arms raised for balance (about 50 per cent of babies walk by 13 months). • May bottom shuffle or bear walk. • Crawls up stairs and comes down backwards (still unsafe).	 *Mature pincer grasp* • Throws objects deliberately and watches them fall. • Will clap hands and wave bye-bye. • Can hold a crayon in a palmer (whole hand) grasp and turn several pages of a book at once. • Shows preference for one hand but uses either.
15 months	• Walks alone, feet wide apart with arms raised to keep balance. • Falls easily, especially upon stopping. • Cannot avoid obstacles and bumps into them. • Can sit from standing. • Can get from sitting to standing without help of furniture. • Can kneel without support. • May climb forwards into an adult chair, then turn round. • Can throw a ball weakly but may fall over.	• Enjoys playing with small blocks or bricks, will often spend time putting them in and out of a container. • Can build a two-brick tower. • Can hold a spoon, but will put it into mouth upside down. • Turns several pages of a book at once. • Points to familiar objects in a book and pats or slaps the page. • Uses index finger constantly to ask for things. • Holds crayon in palmer grasp, scribbling back and forwards on the page. • Shows a preference for one hand but will use either one.
18 months	• Walks confidently without arms out for balance. • Can stop without falling.	• Very fine pincer grasp to pick up small objects.

Age	Gross motor skills	Fine motor skills
18 months	• Can squat to the floor to pick up objects. • Tries to kick a ball, often with success. • Will climb forwards into an adult chair, turning round to sit. • Can run, but often falls, bumping into objects. • Can walk up stairs with hands held. • Likes push-pull toys. If they get stuck behind anything, however, child will try to bully toy free, getting frustrated if it is not coming. • May walk down stairs with hand held.	• Tripod grasp is beginning to develop for holding a crayon. • Scribbles over and back with random dots. • Can build a tower of three or more bricks. • Tries to thread large beads, sometimes succeeding.
2 years	• Can run safely. • Can stop and start easily. • Can squat easily, picking up toy and standing without using hands. • Can walk up and down stairs holding on – two feet to a step. • Can ride a small tricycle by pushing it along with feet – cannot yet use pedals. • Climbs onto furniture. • Tries to kick a ball, but usually walks into it. • Can throw a ball overhand, but not yet catch it.	• Uses preferred hand to hold a pencil and will draw circles, lines and dots. • Can use fine pincer grasp to do complex tasks, e.g. remove clothing from doll or action figure. • Can build a tower of six or more bricks. • Turns pages singly in a book.
2 ½ years	• Stands on tiptoe when shown how to do so. • Walks up stairs confidently and (usually) downwards holding the rail – two feet to a step. • Pushes and pulls large wheeled toys but may have difficulty steering around objects. • Can climb nursery apparatus. • Jumps with both feet together from a low step. • Kicks a large ball, but gently and lopsidedly.	• Can hold a pencil in their preferred hand, with an improved tripod grasp. • Can build a tower of seven or more cubes using their preferred hand. • Can imitate horizontal line and copy T and V as well as draw a circle.
3 years	• Walks alone up stairs with alternating feet and down stairs, two feet to a step. • Usually jumps from bottom step. • Climbs nursery apparatus with agility. • Can turn around obstacles and corners while running and also while pushing and pulling large toys. • Walks forwards, backwards, sideways, etc., hauling large toys with complete confidence. • Rides tricycle, using pedals, and can steer it around wide corners. • Can stand and walk on tiptoe. • Stands momentarily on one (preferred) foot when shown.	• Can pick up very small objects, e.g. thread. • Can build a tower of nine 3 ½-inch cubes – uses hands co-operatively. • Threads large wooden beads on a shoelace. • Can close fist and wiggle thumb in imitation, right and left. • Holds pencil in preferred hand near point between first two fingers and thumb and uses it with good control.

Age	Gross motor skills	Fine motor skills
3 years (cont'd)	• Sits with feet crossed at ankles. • Can throw a ball overhand and catch a large ball on or between extended arms. Kicks a ball forcibly.	• Copies circle, also V, H and T and can imitate cross. • Draws man with head and usually indication of one or two other features or parts. • Enjoys painting with a large brush on easel, covering whole paper with wash of colour or paining primitive 'pictures' which are (usually) named after production. • Cuts with child scissors.
4 years	• Walks (or runs) alone up and down stairs, one foot to a step in adult fashion. • Can turn sharp corners. • Can climb ladders and other playground apparatus. • Can stand, walk and run on tiptoe. • Expert rider of tricycle, negotiating sharp U-turns easily. • Stands on one (preferred) foot for three to five seconds and can hop on preferred foot. • Arranges and picks up objects from floor by bending from waist with knees extended. • Sits with knees crossed. • Shows increasing skill in ball games – throwing, catching, bouncing, kicking, etc., including use of bat or tennis racquet. • Builds tower of 10 or more cubes, may construct bridges, etc.	• Picks up and can replace very small items, e.g. crumbs, with each eye covered separately. • Threads small beads to make necklaces, if adult threads needle. • Holds pencil with good control in adult fashion. Copies X as well as V, H, T and O. • Draws a man with head, legs and trunk and (usually) arms and fingers • Draws a recognisable house. • Beginning to name drawings before production.
5 years	• Can walk easily in a straight line. • Runs lightly on toes. • Has increased agility – can run, dodge, climb and skip. • Good balance; can stand on one foot for 10 or so seconds. • Some may ride a bicycle without stabilisers. • Shows good co-ordination playing ball games and can dance rhythmically to music. • Skips on alternate feet. • Can hop a few metres on each foot separately. • Grips strongly with either hand. • Can bend and touch toes without flexing knees.	• Good control in writing and drawing with pencils. • Copies square and at 5½ can draw a triangle, also letters V, T, H, O, X, L, A, C, U and Y. • Writes a few letters spontaneously. • Draws recognisable man with head, trunk, legs, arms and facial features. • Draws house with door, windows and chimney.

Age	Gross motor skills	Fine motor skills
5 years (cont'd)	• Can play a variety of ball games with considerable ability, including those requiring appropriate placement or scoring according to accepted rules.	• Colours pictures neatly, staying within lines. • Counts fingers on one hand with index finger of other. • Can construct elaborate models using kits such as Duplo. • Can assemble jigsaws with interlocking pieces. • Can use a knife and fork competently, but may still need to have meat cut up for them.
6 years	• Can run and jump, and can kick a football up to 6 metres (18 feet). • Can hop easily with good balance. • Can catch and throw balls with accuracy. • Can ride a two-wheeled bicycle, possibly without stabilisers. • Can skip in time to music, alternating feet.	• Can build elaborate constructions with building blocks, etc. • Can hold a pencil in adult fashion. • Able to write letters of similar size. • Can write their last and first names in a legible fashion.

Development of gross and fine motor skills (six to 12 years) (FETAC Level 6 only)

During the middle years, children's motor abilities continue to develop. Children become stronger, faster and have better co-ordination. Children derive pleasure from testing what they can do with their bodies and from learning new skills. A feature of children's play between six and eight is rough-and-tumble play where children run around chasing, hitting and wrestling each other. This type of play allows them to assess their relative strength against other children. In western culture, rough-and-tumble play is more common among boys, but this gender difference is not seen elsewhere. Blurton-Jones and Konner (1973), for example, found that among bush children in Botswana girls and boys played in very similar ways.

The amount of rough-and-tumble play that children are involved in decreases from the age of seven, when games with rules take over. Gender differences emerge as children grow towards puberty, with boys' gross motor skills tending to become more developed. These differences can be attributed to boys' increased physical strength, but differences in cultural expectations are also a very significant factor.

Fine motor skills are perfected when increased myelination of the neurons of the nervous system allows messages to travel more quickly from neuron to neuron. By age six or seven most children can carry out tasks that require quite complex fine motor skills, such as tying shoe laces, closing buttons or other fastenings and buttering bread. Handwriting becomes smaller and letters more evenly sized. By 12 years most children have developed fine motor skills to a level similar to that of adults; in fact children have a much greater capacity at or before this age for learning new fine motor skills such as playing a musical instrument. While boys generally outperform girls in terms of gross motor skills the opposite is the case with fine motor skills; for example, girls usually have better handwriting.

Environmental factors – effects of family, society and culture on physical development

As with other areas of development, environmental factors have an influence on the development of physical skills. Cultural differences are seen even with the most basic skills, for example, African babies tend to walk at an earlier age (two to three months earlier) than either white or Asian babies. These differences could be related to genetic factors, or to the fact that in some African cultures physical skills such as crawling or standing are actively taught. In contrast, it is usual in some cultures, such as the Yucatan Peninsula in Mexico or the Algonquin culture in Quebec, Canada, for babies to be swaddled and strapped onto cradle boards for much of the day. This slows down development of gross motor skills such as walking, but only temporarily. Interestingly, Navajo (Native American) babies are swaddled and strapped onto cradle boards also, but Navajo babies walk at roughly the same time as white North American babies. This would seem to suggest

Baby strapped onto a cradle board

a hereditary or genetic reason for early or late development of fundamental physical skills.

Changes in the nature of Irish society have had an impact on children's physical development in both positive and negative ways. Many children are given opportunities today that the majority of people from earlier generations did not have. The array of physical activities available promoting gross motor skills is considerable – athletics clubs, heated swimming pools, soccer clubs (with all-weather pitches), Gaelic clubs, martial arts, boxing clubs, dance classes, tennis clubs, golf clubs etc. Here children gain physical strength and fitness as well as developing co-ordination. In terms of fine motor skills, many children learn a musical instrument or perhaps take art and craft classes, particularly during the summer months. While some of these activities are costly, many cost very little and can therefore theoretically be accessed by all children in society. On the other hand, studies such as Growing Up in Ireland, mentioned earlier, highlight the other side of our modern society. Modern children spend much more time than those of previous generations engaged in passive activities, for example 15 per cent of nine-year-old boys spend more than three hours watching television per weekday (more at weekends). Thirty-five per cent of nine-year-olds have a games console in their bedroom and 75 per cent of children are driven to school.

There are differences between socio-economic groups with regard to exercise patterns. Children of unskilled parents spend the most time at sedentary activities and the least time physically exercising. This has an effect on physical development – some children are not availing of sports and activities that promote their co-ordination and overall physical development. Many (as discussed earlier) are becoming overweight and obese and therefore find it more difficult to exercise and improve their gross motor skills.

Gender differences in the development of gross motor skills (boys tend to be more advanced than girls) not only reflect boys' greater physical strength, but also the value society places on boys' and girls' participation in sport.

Promoting gross and fine motor skills (zero to six years)

Zero to one month

- Plenty of physical contact – breastfeeding is best.
- Lots of facial expression – smiling, etc.
- Talk and sing to the baby.
- Baby massage.
- Mobiles with bright primary colours, e.g. Lamaze toys and mobiles use bright colours with pronounced patterns. Babies' eyesight is very poor at this stage and it is believed that these toys are more stimulating for them than more muted colours, e.g. pastels.
- Baby gyms.

A Lamaze toy

Three months

- Offer toys that can be held as well as looked at, e.g. a light colourful rattle that makes a noise.
- Sing songs with the baby on your knee.
- Baby gym of toys strung over cot will encourage the baby to reach out.

- Provide opportunities for exercise – allow the baby to lie on a mat in a warm room without clothes or nappy on so they can move their limbs freely, without restriction.
- Baths that provide support for the baby's head and body allow freedom of movement at bath time. Never leave babies or young children unattended in the bath.

Six months

- Provide bricks to hold and bang together.
- Offer nesting and stacking toys.
- Babies love placing toys such as blocks into containers and removing them again.
- Give babies paper to tear and rattle.
- Offer objects to grasp and that are safe to put in the mouth to explore.
- Offer finger foods – always under supervision.
- Allow babies to experiment with the texture of their food with their fingers.
- Give babies a plastic mirror to look at their own reflection.
- Play clap hands and peek-a-boo, encourage babies to wave bye-bye.
- Play finger rhymes such as this little piggy and round and round the garden.
- Allow babies to bang on upturned saucepans with wooden spoons.

Nine months

- Roll a small ball towards the baby for them to catch as they sit.
- Bathtime can be fun, so provide bath toys to fill, pour and squeeze.
- Many of the toys suitable at six months are even more suitable now, e.g. stacking and nesting toys, blocks, Duplo, saucepans, cardboard boxes.

Twelve months

- Push-pull toys are great for babies who are almost walking.
- Sit-on toys to propel with the feet.
- Small slides and climbing frames.
- Balls to throw, roll and follow.
- Bath toys to fill, pour and squeeze.
- Continue to play action games, e.g. clap hands and peek-a-boo.
- A treasure basket is enjoyable for this age group and older – fill a box or basket with interesting but safe objects, e.g. a brightly coloured block, a lemon, a piece of soft fabric, squeaky toy, etc. Allow the baby to explore.
- Shape sorters.
- Thick, non-toxic crayons to make marks on paper.

- Board books to point at and turn pages.
- Bricks and blocks to stack and build.

Fifteen months

- Large beads and lace with knot on the end to thread.
- Crayons and paper to make marks on.
- Bricks and blocks to stack and play with.
- Child's spoon and fork at mealtimes to practise feeding.
- Bath toys to fill, pour and squeeze.
- Picture books with familiar objects to point at – books should be robust to allow the baby to turn pages easily.

Eighteen months

- Closely supervised sand and water play – containers for pouring and filling, spoons, etc.
- Push-pull toys.
- Finger and foot painting.
- Crayons and paper for drawing.
- Children should be involved in daily cleaning routines, e.g. put dirty clothes in laundry basket.
- Threading beads.
- Large piece jigsaws.
- Bricks and blocks.

Two years

Note: All of the activities suggested for 18 months are also suitable at two years.

- Simple ball games, e.g. gently kicking the ball to and fro.
- Provide a tricycle – will be able to push themselves along but cannot use pedals yet.
- Give children pencils and paper to draw on.

Three years

- Ball games, e.g. football and donkey, are enjoyed.
- Dolls and prams are also enjoyed and develop both gross and fine motor skills, e.g. pushing pram – avoiding obstacles, removing and putting on doll's clothes.
- Provide space for toddlers to ride their tricycles and other push-pull toys.
- Provide pencils, colouring pencils, paint, glue, bits and pieces for sticking, etc.

- Provide shape outlines and children's scissors (make sure to have left-handed pairs available).
- Provide construction toys such as Lego.

Four years

- Provide jigsaw puzzles with thick pieces and allow time for completion.
- Painting and collage activities.
- Use of malleable materials – clay and play dough encourage development of the finger muscles.
- Give the child plenty of writing tools and paper, e.g. old diaries, to encourage 'writing'.
- Provide 'props' for imaginative play, e.g. kitchen sets, dress-up clothes, farm animals and equipment.
- Encourage sand and water play – provide equipment to make play as rich as possible.

Five years

Note: All the activities listed above for four years are also suitable at five years.
- Encourage games such as skipping and hopscotch.
- Play ball games – some children are quite skilled, even at this stage.
- Provide plenty of art and writing materials.
- Gardening is a very useful activity.
- Provide space for cycling (most can cycle using stabilisers).

Six years

- Some children learn to ride a two-wheeled bicycle at this stage without stabilisers. Provide plenty of flat space for them to do so.
- Encourage ball games.
- Encourage dance and rhythm movement to music.
- Provide more complex construction toys such as Mechano, Kinex or Bionicles. Children may have to follow fairly complex instructions for correct assembly or may just create their own objects.
- Provide plenty of art and writing materials.

Promoting gross and fine motor skills (six to 12 years) (FETAC Level 6 only)

- Where possible encourage children to walk or cycle to school (under supervision).
- School yards and playgrounds should be equipped and resourced to encourage children to be physically active at lunchtime. Children should not be kept inside except when the weather is very wet. Parents should ensure children have warm outdoor clothing to enable them to play outside in cold weather.
- Physical education should be a very valued part of the school curriculum. Schools should provide a variety of physical education classes to accommodate children's different needs and interests.
- Parents should encourage their children to take part in extracurricular physical activities outside of school time.
- Parents should be positive and show an interest in what their child is doing, for example, by attending matches and asking their children about the new skills they are learning. It is important, however, that parents do not become too competitive or negative as this can discourage many children from playing sports for life.
- Parents should limit the time their children spend at passive activities such watching television or playing computer games. It is recommended that children should not play computer games at all during the school week.

- Parents can encourage their children's gross and fine motor skills by having them help with tasks around the house, such as making beds, cleaning, cooking and laundry work, e.g. folding clothes.

- Many schools have reintroduced spending time perfecting children's handwriting. This is a good idea if it is done as part of meaningful and interesting activities.
- Creative art and craft activities are useful for the promotion of fine motor skills. Children in this age group enjoy sculpture, jewellery making, collage, drawing, painting and working with clay.
- Traditional crafts such as knitting and sewing are excellent for the promotion of fine motor skills. In the past these skills were a significant part of the primary school curriculum. As this is not now the case, these skills need to be taught at home. The current economic recession is seeing a new interest in these crafts as people begin once again to make and mend their own clothes.
- Playing a musical instrument is beneficial in many ways – development of fine motor skills, development of ability to concentrate and persevere, development of mathematical skills etc. While private music lessons are expensive, many towns around Ireland have concert and marching bands that are not so costly.

Sensory and perceptual development

What can a newborn see? Do babies in intensive care units feel pain? Are our tastebuds all the same at birth, with likes and dislikes for certain foods as a result of our environment? How many sensations can a young baby process at one time? Do newborns recognise their mother's voice? The development of sensation and perception has long been the subject of research by developmental psychologists.

Sensation is when information reacts with the sensory receptors in the eyes, ears, nose, tongue and skin. Sensation means picking up information about the environment through the senses. **Perception** is interpreting that information, e.g. lemon juice tastes sour, that ball is red. Perception involves the brain.

Research methods

Because babies and younger children cannot say what they see, hear, taste, smell or feel, researchers have had to come up with a variety of different ingenious devices to study infant sensation and perception. Robert Fantz (1963), for example, found that infants gazed at different things for different amounts of time, depending on how interested they were in them. He devised a looking chamber. Babies lay on their backs at the bottom of the chamber and were shown various visual materials presented on discs at the top of the chamber. The researcher could look through a peephole at the top of the chamber, observing how long infants looked at various visual materials. This is known as the **visual preference method.** Other researchers have conducted research based on the concept of **habituation and dishabituation.** All of us, including infants, attend longer to something that we have not seen or heard before than to something we are familiar with (consider people who live beside train tracks and no longer hear the trains). This fact has been used to demonstrate that infants can tell the difference between new and old material presented to them. **High-aptitude sucking,** whereby infants show preferences for certain things by sucking rapidly on a non-nutritive nipple, has been used by a number of researchers, e.g. DeCasper and Spence (1986). **The orienting response and tracking** is another method used whereby the infant's head and eye movements are closely observed to evaluate his or her response to various stimuli.

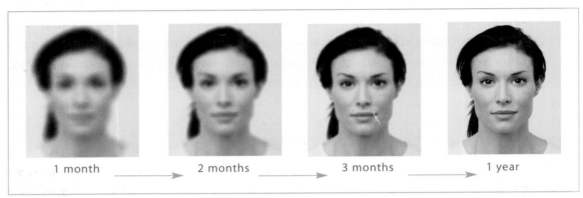

A human face as seen at one, two and three months and one year

Vision

Because the muscles and lenses of the eyes are still developing, newborns have very poor eyesight, estimated to be 20/640 (normal vision is 20/20). This means that something viewed by a newborn at 20 feet is the same as an adult with normal vision viewing it at 260 feet. By six months, vision is believed to be 20/40. Infants show a preference for the human face (particularly their mother's) as little as 12 hours after birth. By three months, infants can distinguish male from female faces, between different ethnic groups and match faces to voices. At birth, infant colour vision is limited, but by four months, they can see colour and show a preference for strong, vivid colours. (It is strange, therefore, that many toys and accessories for young babies are made in pastel colours.) In terms of pattern, Fantz (1963) found that babies as young as two or three months show a preference for vivid patterns, especially patterns that resemble the human face.

Eleanor Gibson and Richard Walk (1960), using their famous visual cliff experiment, sought to find out whether infants could perceive depth or not. Up until this, it was believed that infants could not perceive depth and therefore would not be able to tell if there was a drop, e.g. down a

The Gibson and Walk visual cliff

set of stairs. In their laboratory, Gibson and Walk constructed a miniature cliff with a drop-off covered with glass. They placed infants on the edge of the visual cliff and asked the infants' mothers to try to coax them across. Most infants would not crawl out onto the glass, indicating that they could perceive depth.

Up until approximately four to five years, most children are long-sighted (they cannot see well close up), which is why young children often sit very close to the TV or hold books very close to their face. In addition, until age four or five, children's eye muscles have not developed enough for them to be able to follow letters across a page, which is why many children use their finger to help their eyes track words when they begin reading.

Eye defects

Short-sightedness

Short-sighted children can see things close up, but have difficulty with objects that are far away, such as the blackboard. It normally shows itself between six and 10 years of age and can become worse quite rapidly. It is often noticed because children are slow taking down things from the board, despite normal reading and writing ability. Children need to wear glasses if they are to be able to fully participate in classroom activities.

Long-sightedness

Long-sighted children can see objects far away but close objects will seem blurred. It is less common and more difficult to detect than short-sightedness. Children may appear to lack interest or be lazy.

Strabismus (squint)

If a child has strabismus, commonly called a squint, their eyes look in different directions. One eye is much stronger than the other and is used predominantly for seeing. If the squint is not treated – usually by patching the strongest eye or wearing special glasses – the child can go blind in the 'lazy' eye. A mild squint is normal in very young babies because their eye muscles are still weak. A squint persisting after six weeks or developing later should be checked by an eye specialist.

Colour blindness

Colour blindness is much more common in boys (8 per cent) than girls (0.4 per cent). The most common is red-green colour blindness, where people cannot distinguish red from green. People are not usually treated for colour blindness, but are prohibited from entering certain professions, e.g. pilots.

Astigmatism

There are different forms of astigmatism. With the most common form, the eye is shaped like a rugby ball instead of the normal football shape. This defect makes things appear blurred or out of shape. It can be corrected with glasses.

Blind and partially sighted

Very few people are completely blind. Children can be blind from birth or develop blindness later as a result of accidents or infections. Children who are termed partially sighted have vision that is poor enough to be considered a substantial disability. All areas of development are more challenging for a child who is blind or partially sighted. For example, eye contact may not be possible, an important skill for both emotional and social development, and they cannot learn by watching others, which is important for both cognitive and social skills. In addition, language development may be more difficult, as a child cannot point to cows, fields, etc. and ask what they are.

How we hear

Sound waves are picked up from the environment around us by the pinna – the part of the ear attached to the outside of the head. These sound waves travel along the external auditory canal (ear canal) to the tympanic membrane (ear drum) causing it to vibrate.

Three small bones are then activated by the eardrum – the malleus (commonly called the hammer), incus (commonly called the anvil) and stapes (commonly called the stirrup). The malleus is the bone touching the ear drum. It vibrates, amplifying the sound and passing the vibrations on to the incus and finally the stapes.

The stapes is attached to the cochlea which is a snail-shell-shaped structure filled with fluid. The vibrations cause this fluid to move, stimulating millions of tiny hair cells present on the inside of the cochlea. This causes an electrical message to be passed to the cochlear nerve which travels to the brain to be interpreted as sound.

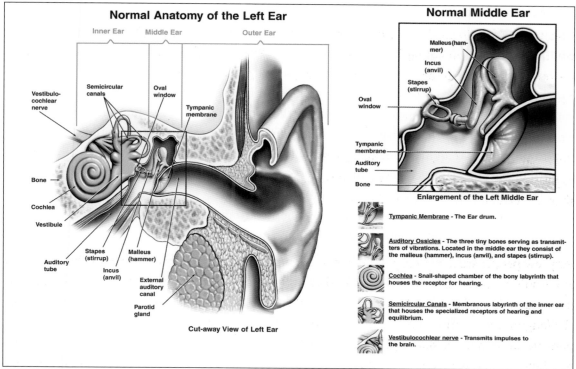

Structure of the ear

Hearing impairment

Approximately one in every 1,000 children born in Ireland has a severe hearing impairment. There are three basic types of impairment: conductive hearing impairment, sensori-neural hearing impairment and mixed impairment.

Conductive impairment occurs when sound is blocked from entering the inner ear. The cause of the blockage occurs either in the outer or middle ear and loss may be temporary. It can be caused by:

- Middle-ear infections.
- A perforated eardrum.
- Earwax or other obstructions, e.g. a bead, in the ear canal.
- Unusual bone growth (otosclerosis) in the ear.
- Thick fluid build-up in the middle ear as a result of persistent ear infections, sometimes called 'glue ear'.
- Head injury damaging the outer or middle ear.

Sensori-neural hearing impairment is caused by problems with the nerves connecting the inner ear to the brain, the inner ear itself, or the areas of the brain that process sound. Sensori-neural hearing loss can be mild, moderate or severe, including total deafness.

The most common reason for sensori-neural hearing loss is the malfunction of the hair cells in the cochlea of the ear. These tiny hair cells pick up vibrations caused by sound entering the inner ear and send a sensory message to the brain via the cochlear nerve. The brain then interprets this as a particular sound. If the hair cells are not functioning properly the vibrations will not be sensed properly and an inadequate message will be sent to the brain. Hair cells may be abnormal at birth or become damaged after birth.

The most usual causes of sensori-neural hearing loss are:

- Genetic – some forms of deafness can be inherited from parents.
- Infections such as meningitis, measles, mumps in infants and children.
- Rubella, herpes, syphilis, chlamydia, HIV and AIDS can be passed to the foetus during pregnancy or to the newborn during the birthing process. All of these can cause deafness (among other things).
- Approximately 60 per cent of children with Foetal Alcohol Syndrome (FAS) have some degree of hearing loss resulting from their mother's drinking.
- Trauma at birth and premature birth (approximately 5 per cent of premature babies experience hearing loss).
- Head injuries after birth, e.g. falls, accidents.
- Prolonged exposure to noise.
- Brain tumours.
- Ototoxic drugs (drugs that can cause damage to the ear). These include some antibiotics, e.g. Gentamicin and Tobramycin, loop diuretics (used to treat patients with kidney problems), some chemotherapy drugs, e.g. Cisplatin and Carboplatin. These drugs do not cause loss of hearing in the vast majority of patients, and the reason why they do in some is not fully understood.

As the name suggests, **mixed impairment** is a mixture of both sensori-neural and conductive impairment.

Taste and smell

Newborn babies can tell the difference and do show a preference for what we would consider pleasant smells and seem to dislike unpleasant ones such as rotten eggs. When babies as young as six days are given the choice of smelling their mother's used breast pad or a clean one, they will turn their heads towards the used one. Newborns do not do this, demonstrating that babies are learning about different smells from very early on. In terms of taste, babies (by studying their facial expressions) are able to tell the difference between sweet and sour solutions. It is thought, however, that later food likes and dislikes are as a result of environmental influences and that children are not born liking or disliking certain foods. This is why children should be exposed to a wide variety of food tastes and textures and adults should not let children observe their own fussy eating patterns.

Touch and pain

For many years, it was widely believed that a newborn's nervous system was not yet developed enough to experience pain. Doctors routinely operated on newborns without anaesthesia. This is now known to be false – newborns *do* feel pain. They may forget about it and stop crying as soon as the pain ceases, but they still feel it. In some cultures, male circumcision is carried out when the baby is three days old. It is usually done without anaesthesia because the risk of giving an anaesthetic at that age is too great. Babies generally cry intensely during circumcision, but usually stop immediately after it is completed and fall into a deep sleep afterwards.

Observing and recording children's physical growth and development

Parents and professionals who care for and work with young children have a responsibility for their well-being. As part of this responsibility, children's growth and development should be systematically observed and recorded so that our expectations of the child are realistic and within their capabilities, that we provide activities and opportunities for them to stimulate the next stage of development and so that children who are not making progress are quickly identified and the appropriate interventions are put in place.

Careful observations and assessments are best carried out over a period of a time in an environment where the child feels at ease, e.g. home or playgroup. Unfortunately, while public health nurses carry out home visits during the first few weeks after birth, most developmental check-ups carried out in Ireland are carried out in clinics that are unfamiliar to the child.

Physical development is usually recorded by using either **developmental checklists** or **centile charts.**

Developmental checklists

Developmental checklists are generally used with children from zero to six years old. They list the norms for the various developmental areas for each age group. Children are observed and tasks are required of them at different ages and their development is compared to the checklist. The purpose of the checklist is to give a general picture of the child's development, thus screening for potential areas of concern.

Centile charts

Developmental centile charts are charts that have been devised after studying the developmental patterns of thousands of children. They compare the growth developmental progress of individual children against that of the 'average' child. Children's height, weight, etc. is expressed as a centile, e.g. a child in the 95th centile for height would be taller than 95 per cent of children his or her age.

How Aistear promotes physical growth and development

While all of Aistear's four themes (see Chapter 1) promote physical development, **Aim 2** of the theme **Well-being** does so very directly. The table below shows what Aistear sets out to do in this area of the early years curriculum. Early years workers provide unstructured and structured play opportunities designed to fulfil these aims and learning goals.

Theme: Well-being	
Aim	**Learning goals**
Aim 2: Children will be as healthy and fit as they can be.	In partnership with the adult, children will: 1. gain increasing control and co-ordination of body movements 2. be aware of their bodies, their bodily functions, and their changing abilities 3. discover, explore and refine gross and fine motor skills 4. use self-help skills in caring for their own bodies 5. show good judgment when taking risks 6. make healthy choices and demonstrate positive attitudes to nutrition, hygiene, exercise, and routine.

(NCCA 2009: 17)

Sample observation

Observation 1: Physical Development

Date of observation: 20 October 2013

Time observation started and finished: 09.30–12.30 (3 hours)

Number of children present: 3

Number of adults present: 1 staff member and 1 student (observer)

Permission obtained from: Supervisor

Description of setting: This observation took place in a large purpose-built community crèche. It caters for children from six months to school-going age and also provides an after-school service. The crèche is open from 8 a.m. to 6 p.m., Monday to Friday, and caters for up to 65 children at a time. Groups are divided according to age – babies, wobblers, toddlers, preschool and after-school. Each group has their own purpose-built room. There is a large all-female staff.

Immediate context: This observation took place in the baby room. It is bright and airy with a separate sleep room attached. The room can accommodate a total of six babies, but today there are only three babies in. The room is supplied with a good variety of colourful toys.

Brief description of the child observed: TC is a female aged six months and one week old. She is new to the crèche – this is her first full week in attendance. She is a large baby who eats and sleeps well. Her mother has her in a very good routine.

Aim of observation: The aim of this observation is to observe TC throughout the morning in order to assess her physical development.

Rationale: It is important to observe children in order to plan developmentally appropriate activities for them.

Method: Checklist.

Media used: Typed checklist obtained from Flood (2013) and pen.

Observation

Directions

Put a ✓ beside items you have observed and an ✗ beside those skills that you observed TC cannot yet master. Put N/O beside items you have not had the opportunity to observe.

Item		Evidence	Date
Prone: Can lift head and chest well clear of the floor, supporting themselves with outstretched arms – hands flat on the floor	✓	TC lifted head and chest well clear of floor when she was placed on play mat after nappy change	20/13
Prone: Can roll over from front to back and (usually) from back to front	✓	Rolled from front to back when placed on play mat – did not appear to try to roll back	20/13
Prone: May pull knees up in an attempt to crawl but will slide backwards	N/O		
Supine: Will lift head to look at feet	✓	Lifted head to look at feet during nappy change	20/13
Supine: May lift arms in a request to be lifted	✗	Does not do this despite staff member putting their arms out to TC to encourage her to do so on several occasions	20/13
Supine: Will kick strongly using alternate feet	✓	Kicked strongly during nappy change and when sitting in baby chair	20/13
Supine: May lift up legs and grasp one foot or both, attempting to put them in mouth	✓	Does lift up legs but did not put foot in mouth while lying under play gym	20/13
Sitting: Held sitting, back will be straight and head firmly erect	✓	After bottle, sits up with head held firmly erect	20/13
Sitting: May sit alone momentarily, but is likely to topple and will not put hands out to break fall	N/O		
Sitting: When hands grasped, will brace shoulders and pull themselves to sit	N/O		
Standing: Enjoys bearing weight and will bounce up and down	✓	Bounced on carer's knee while looking towards window	20/13
Standing: May demonstrate the parachute reflex – when held in the air and whooshed downwards, will straighten and separate legs and fan out toes	N/O		
Uses palmer grasp to grab objects of interest	✓	Used palmer grasp to hold small, flat, soft toy rabbit	20/13
Transfers toys from hand to hand	✓	Transfers toy rabbit jerkily from hand to hand	20/13
Puts toys and other objects in their mouth to explore them	✓	Sucks and bites down on toy rabbit	20/13

Structure of evaluations

As with all reports, evaluations have a beginning, a middle and an end.

Beginning:

- Restate your aims.
- State whether you think each aim was achieved and why.
- Give a general statement of your findings.

Middle:

You should make three or four strong points. Describe what you found and back each point up with theory.

End:

Restate your aim and summarise the points made in the 'middle' section.

Sample evaluation

The aim of this observation was to observe TC, a six-month-old baby girl, throughout the morning in order to assess her physical development. I feel that this aim was achieved very well because the observation was conducted over the entire morning and so allowed me to observe TC for a significant period of time. Generally I found that TC's physical development was within the norms for her age.

In terms of gross motors skills, i.e. use of the large muscles of the body, TC can lift her head and chest up off the floor when lying in the prone position and did so when lying on the play mat after her nappy change. On the play mat she showed she was able to roll from front to back, but did not roll from back to front. TC is making no attempt to crawl yet while in the prone position, which some babies of her age may do (Sheridan 1997). In the supine position, she does lift her head up to look at her feet and kicks strongly using alternate feet during her nappy change. While lying under the play gym, when she got tired of reaching for the dangling objects with her hands, she began playing with her own feet but did not attempt to put them in her mouth. This is not to say that she cannot do so, but rather it was just not observed at this time. TC does not lift arms in a request to be lifted, even when carer puts out their arms to her.

While sitting, TC's head is very erect and she likes to look around. I did not get the opportunity to observe whether she could sit alone or brace herself while being pulled to sit. TC does enjoy bearing weight on her legs and bouncing on the carer's knee while looking towards the window. Again, this is in line with developmental norms for a six-month-old according to Flood (2013). I didn't observe TC demonstrating the parachute reflex.

In terms of fine motor skills, TC used the palmer grasp to hold her soft toy rabbit. She transferred it from hand to hand using jerky movements and sucked and bit down on the toy to explore it. This is in line with the developmental norms as outlined by Minett (2005: 135).

At six months, the baby can now grasp an object without it having to be put in her hand, and she uses her whole hand to do so. At this age she picks up everything in her reach with one hand or two, passes it from hand to hand, turns it over and takes it to her mouth.

In summary, TC's physical development in terms of both gross and fine motor skills seems to have reached most of the developmental milestones expected at her age.

Personal learning gained

I feel I learned a great deal from doing this observation. As this is the first one that I have done, I learned a lot about actually carrying out observations – how they are laid out, how you try to be as objective as possible and how you ensure confidentiality. I also learned a good deal about the physical development of a six-month-old. I would never have looked at this topic in such detail before.

Recommendations

- Continue to provide plenty of toys that encourage TC's physical development, e.g. bricks to hold and bang together, nesting and stacking toys, paper to tear and rattle, objects to grasp that are safe to put in the mouth to explore.
- Offer finger foods – always under supervision – and allow babies to experiment with the texture of the food with their fingers.
- So long as babies are in a warm environment, give them time free from their nappies to kick their legs.

References

Flood, E. (2013), *Child Development for Students in Ireland* (2nd edn.). Dublin, Gill & Macmillan.

Minett, P. (2005), *Child Care and Development* (5th edn.). UK: Hodder Arnold.

Sheridan, M., revised and updated by Sharma, A. and Cockerill, H. (1997), *From Birth to Five Years*, (3rd edn.). UK: Routledge.

Signatures

Anne Jones   Date: <u>20/10/2013</u>
Student

Sarah Patterson   Date: <u>20/10/2013</u>
Supervisor

Ellen Hannon   Date: <u>30/10/2013</u>
Tutor

Revision questions

1. What is meant by the cephalocaudal pattern of growth?
2. List three factors that can affect growth rates in children.
3. Outline the significant environmental factors that have been shown to have an effect on physical growth.

4. Describe the onset of puberty in Irish adolescents. (FETAC Level 6 only)

5. What is meant by the brain's plasticity?
6. Describe the basic structure of the brain.
7. What are neurons?
8. When does most brain development occur?
9. There are two conflicting theories regarding how motor development occurs. Describe both of these theories.
10. What is a reflex?
11. Name six primitive reflexes present at birth.
12. At what age do most reflexes disappear and why would it be a concern if they remained significantly beyond that time?
13. Using examples, differentiate between gross and fine motor skills.
14. Outline the significant environmental factors that have been shown to have an effect on the development of gross and fine motor skills.
15. If a baby is lying in the prone position, what does this mean?
16. Describe key milestones that a baby goes through while learning to walk.
17. Describe how physical development can be promoted in (a) a six-month-old, (b) an 18-month-old, and (c) a four-year-old.

18. Describe how physical development can be promoted in an eight-year-old. (FETAC Level 6 only)

19. Differentiate between the terms 'sensation' and 'perception'.
20. Why do children often need to track words with their finger while reading?
21. What is short-sightedness?
22. In terms of hearing impairment, what is (a) sensori-neural impairment, and (b) conductive hearing impairment?
23. What are (a) developmental checklists and (b) centile charts?
24. In what ways does Aistear promote physical development?

Cognitive Development

What is cognitive development?

Cognitive development includes the development of each of the following:

- Imagination.
- Creativity.
- Memory skills.
- Concentration skills.
- Problem-solving skills.
- Concept formation.

Imagination

Imagination is the ability to form mental images of objects or concepts that are not present or that do not even exist yet. Imagination forms the basis of many of the activities that humans find enjoyable, e.g. reading books and storytelling, dance, art, music and design. Closely linked to the concept of imagination are two others – problem solving and original thought. Solving problems in new or original ways requires imagination and should be encouraged in children at every opportunity. Children should be encouraged to use their imagination in their everyday life to discover things for themselves and solve the small day-to-day problems they encounter.

Imaginative play, particularly **symbolic play**, helps children realise that one thing can represent another. For example, a shoe can be a car for small toy figures. This concept is important later on for skills such as reading and writing, where letters have to represent words.

Role play that involves the child becoming somebody or something else also helps develop many other important skills. For example, a child pouring water into cups pretending to be serving coffee in a café is developing their hand–eye co-ordination, their knowledge of volume and their social skills.

Creativity

Creativity is the expression of imaginative ideas in a unique and personal way. Creativity can be expressed in many different ways, e.g. writing stories or poems, creating artwork, making music, dance, cookery and gardening. Being creative is not imitating someone else's ideas. Children often come home from playschool with identical art and craft work; this is not being creative. Children should be given the resources to help them develop their creativity and allowed to go about it themselves. Sometimes adults provide a framework within which children work creatively, but the activity should not be too adult led. Frameworks can be provided in different ways. For example, if a group is working on the theme of autumn, the adult could provide a range of materials in autumn colours.

Memory skills

Memory is a vital part of learning and therefore cognitive development. Memory really involves three tasks: encoding (putting information into storage), storage (retaining information over time) and retrieval (taking information out of storage). The development of memory involves perfecting these three tasks. Whether something is memorised or learned depends on the following.

- How much there is to be learned – if too much information is presented at once, it will overload the working memory (also called the short-term memory) and information will not be encoded at all.
- Whether the new memory is linked to existing information – does the learner already know something about what is being learned? If they do, they are much more able to learn the new information.
- Does the leaner understand what is being learned? Information that is not understood is difficult to memorise.

- Repetition – has the information been repeated often enough for it to stay in the long-term memory?

While infants begin to remember from about six months (Bauer 2007), most adults remember little, if anything, from their first three years of life. This phenomenon is known as **infantile or childhood amnesia** and is thought to be a result of the fact that during these first three years of life, the brain's prefrontal lobes (responsible for remembering events) are immature.

Memory span is another aspect of memory that improves throughout childhood. Memory span refers to the amount of information that can be held and processed in the working or short-term memory at any one time. Generally, memory span increases throughout childhood, from about two items of information at age two, to five items at age seven, to seven items at age 12 through to adulthood. It is important to know this so that too much information is not presented to a young child at one time.

What does this information on memory mean for people working with young children? The example below illustrates how this theory translates into practice.

Lily has planned a series of activities to be presented over the next few weeks to enable the children to recognise the written numbers one to 10.

- Introduce number songs, e.g. 'Five Little Ducks Went Swimming One Day', 'Ten Green Bottles Hanging on a Wall'. As the song is sung, hold up relevant numbers. Later, when children become familiar with the song, give each child a number to hold up at the relevant time.
- Number activities such as lotto, number jigsaws, etc.
- Art activities where children have to decorate a large written number for display around the room.
- Children have to make their favourite number out of play dough and talk about why they like the number.
- Sorting activities where children have to sort groups of items into boxes numbered one to 10, depending on how many items are in the group.
- Movement games whereby children have to get into line depending on the number they are holding.

Concentration skills

Concentration is the skill of focusing your attention on a task. It is a necessary skill for learning to take place and children who do not develop this skill for whatever reason generally struggle in the educational environment, especially as they progress. Children will be encouraged to concentrate if:

- Activities are at the correct level for them – if activities are too difficult or too easy, children will quickly lose concentration.
- Activities are interesting and attractively presented.
- Adults encourage and praise the child's efforts.

Young children have quite short attention spans, so activities should not be too prolonged. Having said this, it is important to help develop children's attention span, so activities should be organised that stretch but do not surpass their ability. As a rule of thumb, a typical attention span is between three and five minutes per year of a child's age, so a two-year-old should be able to stay on task for at least six minutes, a three-year-old for at least nine minutes and so on. Attention span while engaged in passive activities such as watching TV or playing video games is not what is meant here, as children are not being challenged to process information while engaged in these activities.

Concentration skills can and should be encouraged by those who work with young children. Examples of how this may be done are as follows.

- Encourage children to sit and listen to full stories.
- Encourage children to complete activities, e.g. a jigsaw, before moving on to the next one.
- Play games, e.g. board games, that require children to persevere to the end.
- Limit time spent at activities that do not promote concentration skills, e.g. passively watching videos.

Attention deficit (hyperactivity) disorder (ADD and ADHD)

ADD and ADHD are described as neurobehavioural developmental disorders, both of which affect a child's ability to concentrate. Together, they are thought to affect 3 to 5 per cent of the population, and hyperactivity is usually present – ADHD is much more commonly diagnosed than ADD (although this could be because the child with ADD does not draw as much attention to him/herself). Children with ADD and ADHD will show some of the following symptoms. For a diagnosis to be made, the child usually has to show symptoms in more than one situation, e.g. at home, in school and during leisure activities.

Condition	Usual symptoms
ADD	• Is easily distracted, misses details, forgets things and frequently switches from one activity to another. • Has difficulty focusing on one thing. • Becomes bored with a task after only a few minutes, unless they are doing something enjoyable. • Has difficulty focusing attention on organising and completing a task or learning something new. • Has trouble completing or turning in homework, often loses things, e.g. pencils, toys, homework, needed to complete tasks or activities. • Does not seem to listen when spoken to. • Daydreams, becomes easily confused and moves slowly. • Has difficulty processing information as quickly and accurately as others. • Struggles to follow instructions.
ADHD	• Fidgets and squirms constantly. • Talks non-stop. • Dashes around, touching or playing with anything and everything in sight, but only momentarily. • Has trouble sitting still during dinner, school and story time. • Is constantly in motion. • Has difficulty doing quiet tasks or activities. • Is very impatient. • Blurts out inappropriate comments, shows their emotions without restraint and acts without considering the consequences. • Has difficulty waiting for things they want or waiting their turn in games.

If ADD or ADHD is left untreated, these difficulties can have serious long-term consequences for the child in that it can severely interfere with his or her ability to get the most out of education, fulfil his or her potential in the workplace, establish and maintain interpersonal relationships and maintain a positive self-image. ADHD is usually treated with medication.

Problem-solving skills

The ability to figure out and solve problems is another important aspect of cognitive development. When children begin to try to solve problems, they take a **trial and error** approach. If you watch a two-year-old child doing a jigsaw puzzle, they will try to fit each piece in one at a time until they eventually pick the one that fits. An older child may organise the pieces in some way before trying to fit them together, e.g. find the corner and edge pieces or pieces of the same colour first and work from there. This is the next stage in the development of problem-solving skills. Children will begin to identify the problem facing them and work out a possible solution *before* they try anything out. Children begin to be able to mentally predict what may happen. This is called the **hypothesis approach** to problem solving. The children form a hypothesis or idea to be tested based on their knowledge of the world. The greater children's knowledge and experience, the more accurate their hypothesis is likely to be. This is why it is important to expose children to as wide a variety of learning experiences as possible.

Children primarily solve problems using the trial and error approach until they are about two years of age. From this age on, they begin to hypothesise and think about the problems they face before deciding on a course of action. Naturally, the child's ability to hypothesise and consider possible solutions develops with age and depends on the child's experiences.

Concept formation

Concepts are the mental pictures we hold in our heads about the world. There are basically two types of concept: concrete concepts, e.g. dogs, chairs, cars and flowers, and abstract concepts, e.g. justice, fractions and time. Concept formation is a vital part of cognitive development in that it helps us organise and make sense of the world around us. Piaget's work (see below) looked closely at how children form concepts, so this aspect of cognitive development will be dealt with more fully then.

Behaviourist theories of cognitive development

Behaviourists such as **B.F. Skinner (1904–90)** believe that learning is the acquisition of new behaviour through **conditioning**. There are two types of conditioning – classical and operant.

Classical conditioning

The theory of classical conditioning was developed by the physiologist Ivan Pavlov (1849–1936). Pavlov was working on a medical project studying the salivary glands in dogs when he noticed that every time someone appeared in a white lab coat, the dogs began to salivate. They associated the lab coat with food. This then became the focus of his project. He began ringing a bell (which he called the stimulus) each time the dogs were about to be fed, and within a short time the dogs began to salivate (which he called the response) upon hearing a bell. Classical conditioning is when the body automatically responds to a stimulus. Consider this example:

Alan left school at 14, as he absolutely hated it. He couldn't read or write properly, his teachers thought he was stupid and he lived in constant fear of his classmates finding out he was virtually illiterate. Alan never stood in a school again until he was 35 years old and decided he wanted to vote.

As he walked in the door he could feel his heart racing, his hands began to sweat and he felt vaguely sick.

How could Alan's experience be explained in terms of classical conditioning theory?

Operant conditioning

Operant conditioning occurs when behaviour is reinforced by being either rewarded (which increases the likelihood of the behaviour reoccurring) or punished (which decreases the likelihood of the behaviour reoccurring). Learning occurs as a result of this process. Skinner based much of his theory on his work with lab rats and other animals. In his most famous experiment he devised a box called 'Skinner's Box' in which he trained lab rats through operant conditioning to press a lever a certain number of times for food. He was interested in observing the effects of punishment and different reward schedules on the animals' behaviour. What did Skinner find?

- Reward is a much stronger reinforcer than punishment. Punishments have to be quite severe before they will effectively stop an undesired behaviour.
- When a desired behaviour is rewarded, it is repeated.
- The most difficult behaviour to stop is one that has been reinforced irregularly. This has been called the 'slot machine effect'.

For example, a mother tells her six-year-old son that he is not allowed to have crisps before his dinner. Nine times out of 10 she sticks to her rule and does not allow crisps. On the odd occasion, however, if she is busy, she will give him a bag of crisps to keep him quiet until she has time to make the dinner. The boy frequently asks for crisps before dinnertime. Why?

Critics of the behaviourist approach believe that human learning is much more complex than this. They believe that there are many factors other than whether something has been rewarded or punished to be considered.

Constructivist theories of cognitive development – Jean Piaget

Jean Piaget (1896–1980) was a Swiss-born psychologist who, through careful observation of his own three children and many others, developed a theory of cognitive development that changed people's perceptions of how children's minds develop. Piaget believed that children actively construct their own cognitive worlds and are not just passive receivers of information – vessels into which information is poured. Piaget believed that as a result of exposure to the environment around them, children adjust and build their mental structures to suit what they are experiencing, which he called **adaptation**.

Key concepts related to Piaget's theory

- **Schema:** Piaget believed that as the child begins to construct their understanding of the world, the developing brain creates schemas. A schema is a mental structure that represents some aspect of the world. For example, our schema for zebra is of a large four-legged animal with black and white stripes. A schema can also be a mental structure for an action, e.g. how to walk down steps.

- **Assimilation and accommodation:** Children adapt and change their schemas over time. For example, at first a young child may call all vehicles that move on the road 'cars', e.g. cars, vans, trucks, motorbikes and buses. According to Piaget, they fine tune things through two processes – assimilation and accommodation. Assimilation is when children incorporate new information into their existing schemas and accommodation is when children adjust their schemas in light of this new information. Taking the example above of 'cars', as the child experiences more of the world and assimilates more information about vehicles that travel on the road, they fine tune their ideas about what a car is so that it excludes vans (no windows in the back), trucks (too big and no windows in the back), motorbikes (only two wheels and no windows) and buses (too big, too many windows) – this is accommodation.

- **Organisation** is another term used by Piaget and refers to the capacity of the human mind to organise and link or combine different schemas together. For example, a three-year-old child has learned the following schema separately – walking down stairs safely and that liquids spill if their container is not kept upright. He or she will combine both these schema in order to walk down stairs holding a beaker of juice.

- **Equilibrium and disequilibrium:** When a child (or indeed an adult) is exposed to something new about the world that conflicts with their existing ideas, they experience disequilibrium (lack of balance). For example, take a child who in the beginning calls any large four-legged creature a 'cow'. After a while and through experience, the child will begin to notice that something is not quite right with some of their 'cows' (disequilibrium), and they will begin to change their thinking and come up with other categories, such as horses, zebras, etc. Once they have done this, equilibrium is restored. All human beings are motivated to seek equilibrium.

Piaget's stage theory of cognitive development

According to Piaget, individuals go through four stages of cognitive development. He believed that at each stage, a child's reasoning or way of processing information is **qualitatively** different from the stage that went before or comes after, and that it was not just that a younger child possesses less information than an older one. Piaget's four stages are as follows.

1. Sensori-motor stage (zero to two years),
2. Pre-operational stage (two to seven years)
3. Concrete operational stage (seven to 11 years)
4. Formal operational stage (11+ years)

Sensori-motor stage (zero to two years)

During the sensori-motor stage, the infant progresses from a newborn focusing almost exclusively on immediate sensory and motor experiences to the toddler who possesses a capacity for thinking. Piaget detailed development through the first two years of a child's life by observing his own three children, dividing the sensori-motor stage into six sub-stages.

Sub-stage	Age (months)	Characteristics of sub-stage
Reflex activity	0–1	Infants demonstrate innate reflexes, e.g. sucking, grasping and crying.
Primary circular reactions	1–4	Infant repeats actions first encountered by chance, e.g. an infant sucks its thumb by chance and will begin doing so intentionally. Actions all directed at self.
Secondary circular reactions	4–10	Beings to repeat actions that have not originated as reflexes, e.g. kicking toys hanging from a play gym. Interacts with objects in their environment – actions now no longer directed at self exclusively.
Co-ordination of secondary circular reactions	10–12	The baby begins to co-ordinate their schema and actions and they may begin to use tools, e.g. fork and spoon.
Tertiary circular reactions	12–18	Infants actively use trial and error methods to learn about objects. Increased mobility allows them to explore and problem solve.
Internal representation	18–24	Infants begin to be capable of mental action – being able to think about things that are not there in front of them. They begin to be able to use symbols to represent things and people, e.g. a block can become a car. A toddler who sees another toddler pull a playmate's hair may remember this action and do the same thing the following day.

The development of **object permanence** is one of the major feats of the sensori-motor stage. Object permanence is the understanding that objects or people continue to exist even when they cannot be seen, heard or touched. One way of testing for an infant's awareness of object permanence is by showing him or her an interesting toy, then removing the toy from view. If a child has no sense of object permanence, he or she will not look for the toy. At approximately seven months, an understanding of object permanence begins to emerge. Consequently, it is at this time that many babies begin to be upset when their primary carers leave them to be cared for by someone else. This is because when the primary carer leaves, the baby remembers them and misses them in their absence. Previous to this, once the carer was out of sight, they were out of mind.

Pre-operational stage (two to seven years)

During the pre-operational stage, the child does not yet perform **operations.** Operations are internalised actions that allow children to mentally carry out tasks. For example, an operation would be adding two numbers in your head without having to use physical props such as fingers. A child who is capable of operations is also able to mentally reverse actions. During the pre-operational stage, the child is preparing themselves to perform operations. The pre-operational stage is divided into two sub-stages: the symbolic function sub-stage and intuitive thought sub-stage.

Symbolic function sub-stage

This stage occurs between two and four years. During this stage, children become able to represent people and objects when they are not present, using scribble designs to represent people, houses, cars, animals, etc. Two limiting features of this stage are egocentrism and animism. Up to the age of four years, children are believed to be profoundly **egocentric.** This means that they are not capable of viewing things from another's perspective. For example, a young child speaking on the phone will often just nod or shake their head in reply to a question. They cannot consider that the person they are talking to cannot see them, because they can see themselves. **Animism** is another feature of this stage. Animism is the belief that objects have lifelike qualities and are capable of feelings and action. This is why if a child bumps his or her head off the edge of a table, for example, they are comforted somewhat if the table is punished for hurting them – 'Bold table for hurting Molly, bold table!' (adult slapping table).

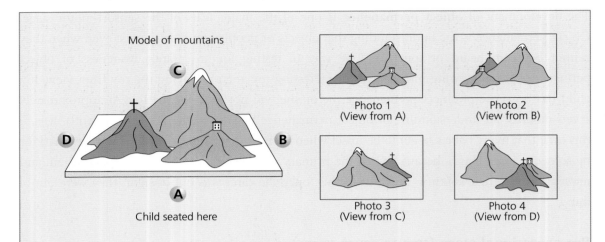

Piaget and his colleague Barbel Inhelder (1969) devised what is now called the 'three mountains task' to investigate young children's egocentrism. They found that children under four years of age had difficulty with the task and concluded from this that they were profoundly egocentric, meaning that they could not see something from another's perspective. During the task, the child walks around a model of three mountains (see above) and becomes familiar with what the mountains look like from different perspectives. The child is then seated on one side of the table (position A) and the experimenter then moves a doll around the table, seating it at positions B, C and D. Each time the doll is moved, the experimenter asks the child to pick out from a series of four photographs what the doll can see. Children under four consistently choose photo 1, believing that the doll can see what they can see. Piaget and Inhelder's findings have been since debated (see criticisms of Piaget on page 109).

Intuitive thought sub-stage (four to seven years)

At this stage, children begin to use primitive reasoning and want to know the answers to all sorts of questions – when? Where? Why? Children are not yet able to understand the principle of cause and effect, e.g. a child is not able to mentally represent what would happen if a car hit them. Another characteristic of this stage is **centration**. Children tend to focus or centre on just one characteristic of an object or idea, thereby showing an inability to **decentre.**

Example: A group of children four to seven years old was shown a picture of a collection of dolls, some with hats on and others without, some male and some female. They would generally be able to answer the following question – How many dolls have hats on? Most, however, would have difficulty answering this question – How many boy dolls have hats on? This is because they have difficulty focusing on two things at once (hat wearing and gender).

Piaget demonstrated children's inability to decentre through his famous **conservation** experiments or tasks. He believed that because children under the age of seven could not decentre, they could not conserve. Conservation means understanding that just because the appearance of something changes, it does not automatically mean its basic properties have changed. Examine the conservation experiments below to further understand this idea.

Type of conservation	Stage 1 of experiment	Stage 2 of experiment	Pre-operational child's likely answer
Volume	Child is shown two identical beakers full of coloured liquid. Child agrees both contain the same amount of liquid.	Child sees experimenter pour liquid from one beaker into a tall thin one – child asked which one has more liquid or are they both the same.	The tall thin one (the child can focus on only one thing – usually focuses on height).
Number	Child is shown two rows of buttons, one directly opposite the other. Child agrees both rows contain the same number of buttons.	Child sees the experimenter spread out one row of buttons – child asked which row contains the most buttons now or are they both the same.	The child will pick the spread-out row.
Mass	Child is shown two identical balls of play dough. Child agrees both balls contain the same amount of play dough.	Child sees experimenter roll one ball into a long sausage shape – child asked which contains the most play dough now or are they both the same.	The child will pick the sausage shape.

Type of conservation	Stage 1 of experiment	Stage 2 of experiment	Pre-operational child's likely answer
Length	Child is shown two sticks, one directly opposite the other. Child agrees both sticks are the same length.	Child sees experimenter push one stick forward – child asked which stick is longer now or are they both the same.	Child will pick the stick that has been pushed forward.

Concrete operational stage (seven to 11 years)

This stage lasts from around age seven to 11. During this stage, children learn to conserve. For example, a child at the concrete operational stage will say when a round ball of clay is transformed into a sausage shape that 'it is longer, but it is thinner' or 'if you change it back into the ball it will be the same again'. In this way, children understand that actions can be reversed. Conservation of number usually occurs first (sometimes as young as five), with conservation of volume last (often not until 10 or 11 years). Children can problem solve at this stage as long as the problems are concrete in nature. For example, Anna is taller than Nina. Anna is smaller than Lily. Who is the smallest? This problem is difficult for a child at the concrete operations stage. However, if the child was given dolls representing Anna, Nina and Lily, they would have no problem answering the question because they have concrete 'props' to help them. This is why many children's maths books nowadays have counters or number lines at the top of the page to aid the concrete thinker.

Formal operational stage (11+ years)

Piaget argued that it was not until this stage that children can reason hypothetically and understand abstract concepts. Ask a child of nine or 10 to explain what the concept 'justice' means – if they have heard the word before, most are likely to explain with a concrete example: 'Justice is when your mother gives out to your brother for scratching your PlayStation game.' Children at the formal operations stage also approach problems in a more logical, systematic way. Give a child at the concrete operations stage a big bunch of keys and ask them to find the one that opens a lock. He or she is most likely to approach the problem in a disorganised way, trying different keys randomly. A child at the formal operational stage, on the other hand, is likely to take an organised, systematic approach. Critics of Piaget, e.g. Shayer and Wylam (1978), say that if children are coached, they can reach the formal operational stage early, concluding that Piaget's stages are not as clearly defined age wise as he proposed.

Criticisms of Piaget's theory

Criticisms of Piaget's theories centre around two main areas. The first is that children may have failed to complete many of his tasks not because they couldn't, but because the tasks were conducted in an environment very strange to the child (laboratory setting). In addition, with many of his experiments, the child was confused about what they were being asked to do because the tasks did not make **human sense** (see Donaldson (1978) below). The second criticism is that Piaget applied his theories quite rigidly and across the board he took no account of the effects of education, training and culture.

Margaret Donaldson's policeman experiment

Margaret Donaldson (1978) described a series of experiments carried out by herself and her colleagues which showed that children as young as three and a half were capable of appreciating another's point of view. In this way, Donaldson sought to oppose Piaget's contention that children less than seven years old were by and large egocentric, a finding supported by his 'three mountains task' described earlier. The Donaldson experiment consists of two 'walls' set up to form a cross, a toy policeman and a boy. The child is asked to help the boy hide from the policeman, so is required to place him where the policeman cannot see him (Donaldson and Hughes 1978). In some versions of the experiment, the boy has to hide from two policemen, so the child has to appreciate two viewpoints other than his or her own.

Donaldson claimed that the 'policeman' task made human sense and that it was realistic and interesting for the child:

'The task requires the child to act in ways which are in line with certain very basic human purposes (escape and pursuit). It makes human sense … in this context, he shows none of the difficulty in "decentring" which Piaget ascribes to him … the "mountains task" is abstract in a psychologically very important sense, in the sense that it is abstracted from all basic human purposes and feelings and endeavours.' (Donaldson 1978: 24)

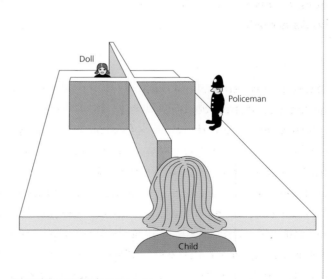

Donaldson's Policeman task

Social constructionist theories of cognitive development – Lev Vygotsky

Lev Vygotsky was born in 1896 in what is now Belarus. Unfortunately, he died of TB aged only 38 in 1934. Like Piaget, Vygotsky believed that children actively construct their knowledge and understanding and are not merely vessels to be filled with facts and information. Unlike Piaget, however, who saw the child as somewhat of a 'lone scientist', Vygotsky emphasised the importance of social relationships (other people) in a child's learning processes. Two particular concepts emerge from Vygotsky's work that are of particular importance to childcare staff: the zone of proximal development and scaffolding.

The zone of proximal development

The zone of proximal development (ZPD) is the area in the middle between what a child can do on their own and what they can do with adult or more able peer assistance. Tasks that children can just about master alone are at the very bottom of their ZPD and those they can master only with assistance are at the top. Tasks that are very easy or very difficult for the child are outside the zone altogether. Vygotsky believed that teaching is about finding each child's ZPD and guiding them along it. Tasks outside the zone – too easy (below) or too difficult (above) – should not be presented, as children will quickly become either bored and uninterested or frustrated and give up.

Scaffolding

Closely linked to the zone of proximal development is Vygotsky's concept of **scaffolding**. He believed that the job of teacher (adult or more able peer) involves providing the correct level of support (scaffolding) to the learning child. When a child is first introduced to something new and challenging (at the top of their ZPD), the adult or more able peer provides a lot of support. The amount of support should lessen as the child becomes more competent. If children are given too much support (the adult half does the task for them), they usually hand over the task to the adult and stop trying themselves (see case study below).

CASE STUDY

St Brigid's crosses made from rushes are traditionally made in Irish primary schools on the first day of February every year. When Sam was in 1st class, his teacher made crosses with them. After a while (the children were working away happily on the crosses), the teacher realised that the crosses the children were making weren't looking much like St Brigid's crosses. As a result, she got the children to line up so that she could tidy them up for them. The children lined up and the teacher redid much of the work the children had done, eventually succeeding in making a whole classroom of very respectable crosses. After class, she wiped her brow and thought to herself that she wasn't going to try that one again, as the crosses were just too difficult for the children. Sam came out of school with his cross. When his mother complimented him on how good it looked, he said, 'Well, teacher sort of did it.' He left the cross in a pocket in the back seat of the car, where it withered and was only found the next time the car was cleaned out. The following year, Sam had a different teacher. He came out of school holding a misshapen cross tied unevenly with elastic bands. His mother asked him if he had done it all himself. He said, 'Well, teacher helped at bit, but mostly I did it.' That evening, Sam asked his mother where he could put the cross. They hung it over a photo in the living room for all to see.

Theories of multiple intelligences

Robert Sternberg's (1949–) triarchic theory of intelligence proposes that intelligence comes in three forms – analytic, creative and practical. Most people tend to be stronger in one than the other two.

Someone with strong **analytic** intelligence finds it easy to analyse, evaluate, compare and contrast. As these are skills that are demanded by our education system, children with strong analytic intelligence tend to do very well in school.

Someone with strong **creative** intelligence has the ability to imagine, invent, design and create. Strong creative intelligence is useful for some subjects at school, such as art and technology, but not as beneficial for others. In our education system, where many subjects are compulsory, children with strong creative intelligence often have to do a lot of subjects that do not particularly play to their strengths. As a result these children frequently do not achieve as well as those with analytic intelligence.

Someone with strong **practical** intelligence is good at doing things, assessing and solving practical problems. Children with strong practical intelligence are generally good at subjects that have a large hands-on element to them, such as technology. As with creative intelligence, because children with strong practical intelligence often have to do a number of subjects that require analytic skills, these children often do not achieve as well as those with analytic intelligence.

Howard Gardner (1943–) believes that there are eight frames of mind or types of intelligence. As with Sternberg's theory, he believes that people are stronger in some of them than others. He also believes that in the right environment all areas can be promoted in children.

Form of intelligence	Strengths
Verbal or linguistic	Good with words and language, can use the written word very effectively, e.g. journalists, actors, authors.
Logical or mathematical	Good with numbers and at noticing patterns. Good at problem solving, e.g. computer programmers.
Bodily or kinaesthetic	Find it easy to develop and perfect new physical skills, e.g. sports people, dentists, surgeons, crafts people.
Visual or spatial	Good at thinking three-dimentionally, e.g. architects and artists.
Naturalist	Understand the natural world, e.g. farmers, landscape gardeners, botanists.
Intrapersonal	Have good self-knowledge and like to work independently, e.g. authors.
Musical or rhythmical	Sensitive to pitch and tone of music, enjoy music and can learn to play easily, good dance rhythm, e.g. musicians, dancers.
Interpersonal	Find it easy to get along with others and work as part of a team, e.g. nurses.

Learning styles

It is widely accepted that in addition to theories of multiple intelligences, people can have varying learning styles. The three most common learning styles are visual, auditory, and kinaesthetic.

Approximately 29 per cent of people are predominantly **visual** learners, meaning they learn best by looking. While studying, visual learners should make notes on post-its or prompt cards, use diagrams, mind maps and flow charts and highlighting pens.

Approximately 34 per cent of learners are predominantly **auditory** learners, meaning they learn best by listening. While studying, auditory learners should read notes onto a recording device and listen back, read information that needs to be learned aloud and get friends or family to ask questions on what they have learned.

Approximately 37 per cent of learners are **kinaesthetic** learners, meaning they learn best by doing. While studying, kinaesthetic learners should walk around while reading work, write notes on post-its and stick them around the room, walking from note to note while learning, run their finger under words.

Environmental factors – effects of family, society and culture on cognitive development

As with other areas of development, the debate regarding the extent to which a child's cognitive development is influenced by nature or nurture is still ongoing. Adoption studies show that children's IQ levels are usually closer to that of their biological parents than that of their adopted parents. Lucurto (1990) did find, however, that when children's environment improved as a result of adoption, on average their IQ rose by 12 points. This would indicate that while cognitive development is certainly highly influenced by genetics, a stimulating environment is vital to enable children to reach their potential. The 'Flynn Effect' (named after James Flynn, an American researcher working in New Zealand) has seen IQ scores rise year on year, among children from all parts of the world. This is largely because modern children receive a better quality of education for much longer than in the past. If a group of present-day children took the Stanford-Binet test as issued to children in 1932, approximately 25 per cent would reach the standard reached by the top 3 per cent of children in 1932.

One of the biggest factors affecting cognitive development and educational attainment in Ireland today is social class. Children from lower socio-economic groups do not, on average, do as well as their middle- and upper-class contemporaries. The reasons for these divisions are complex and varied. Studies such as Nettle (2003) of IQ differences between different socio-economic groups show that children from higher socio-economic groups have higher average IQ scores than children from lower socio-economic groups. IQ is a predictor of educational attainment, so this is one reason put forward by some researchers why children from higher socio-economic groups tend to do better in school.

However, most researchers concentrate on other possible (and very valid) reasons why some children do not succeed as well as others. Children from lower socio-economic groups are more likely to grow up in households where, for example, there are fewer books and other educational materials. As we saw in Chapter 4, children from lower socio-economic groups are less likely to have a balanced diet or take exercise. Perhaps because of parents' experiences at school, some households may not value education and therefore may not be as school-supportive as other parents. There are, of course, many exceptions to these trends. Many children from lower socio-economic groups succeed very well in education and in life. A scheme to provide a year of free pre-school education was initiated in Ireland in 2010 to allow children from all backgrounds to receive a positive early start to their education.

Worldwide there are cultural differences in terms of (1) what sort of cognitive skills are valued, and (2) how they are taught. In more traditional societies practical intelligence is valued, whereas in more industrial societies analytic and creative intelligence can often be more rewarded. In traditional societies there is a greater emphasis on **guided participation** than in industrial societies. With guided participation adults in the community teach children skills required by that community. The child works alongside the adult, learning the necessary skills as they go along. In industrialised societies such as ours, much of a child's education is acquired in educational institutions – pre-schools, schools, colleges and universities.

Promoting cognitive development

There are many ways cognitive development may be promoted.

- Talk and interact with a baby from birth. Try to provide the baby with good routines. Provide a stimulating environment when the baby is awake. Use child-directed speech (motherese).
- Provide plenty of interesting activities for the child – sand and water play, art materials, dress-up clothes, small world toys, jigsaws and other puzzles and construction toys such as Lego. Scaffold their learning but make sure not to help too much.
- Allow children to safely explore the wider environment with visits to the park, beach, zoo, etc.
- Provide plenty of reading and writing materials for children.
- Have children help out with household tasks in a meaningful way – cooking, cleaning, gardening, gathering and sorting laundry, etc.
- Read with and for children and ask them their opinions on what they have read.

- Older children: supervise and support homework in a positive way (FETAC Level 6 only).

How Aistear promotes cognitive development

While all of Aistear's four themes promote cognitive development, the theme **Exploring and thinking** does so very directly. The table below shows what Aistear sets out to do in this area of the early years curriculum. Early years workers provide unstructured and structured play opportunities designed to fulfil these aims and learning goals.

Theme: Exploring and thinking	
Aims	**Learning goals**
Aim 1: Children will learn about and make sense of the world around them.	In partnership with the adult, children will: 1. engage, explore and experiment in their environment and use new physical skills including skills to manipulate objects and materials 2. demonstrate a growing understanding of themselves and others in their community 3. develop an understanding of change as part of their lives 4. learn about the natural environment and its features, materials, animals, and plants, and their own responsibility as carers 5. develop a sense of time, shape, space, and place 6. come to understand concepts such as matching, comparing, ordering, sorting, size, weight, height, length, capacity, and money in an enjoyable and meaningful way.

Aim 2: Children will develop and use skills and strategies for observing, questioning, investigating, understanding, negotiating, and problem-solving, and come to see themselves as explorers and thinkers.	In partnership with the adult, children will: 1. recognise patterns and make connections and associations between new learning and what they already know 2. gather and use information from different sources using their increasing cognitive, physical and social skills 3. use their experience and information to explore and develop working theories about how the world works, and think about how and why they learn things 4. demonstrate their ability to reason, negotiate and think logically 5. collaborate with others to share interests and to solve problems confidently 6. use their creativity and imagination to think of new ways to solve problems.
Aim 3: Children will explore ways to represent ideas, feelings, thoughts, objects, and actions through symbols.	In partnership with the adult, children will: 1. make marks and use drawing, painting and model-making to record objects, events and ideas 2. become familiar with and associate symbols (pictures, numbers, letters, and words) with the things they represent 3. build awareness of the variety of symbols (pictures, print, numbers) used to communicate, and use these in an enjoyable and meaningful way leading to early reading and writing 4. express feelings, thoughts and ideas through improvising, moving, playing, talking, writing, story-telling, music and art 5. use letters, words, sentences, numbers, signs, pictures, colour and shapes to give and record information, to describe and to make sense of their own and others' experiences 6. use books and ICT (software and the internet) for enjoyment and as a source of information.
Aim 4: Children will have positive attitudes towards learning and develop dispositions like curiosity, playfulness, perseverance, confidence, resourcefulness, and risk-taking.	In partnership with the adult, children will: 1. demonstrate growing confidence in being able to do things for themselves 2. address challenges and cope with frustrations 3. make decisions and take increasing responsibility for their own learning 4. feel confident that their ideas, thoughts and questions will be listened to and taken seriously 5. develop higher-order thinking skills such as problem-solving, predicting, analysing, questioning, and justifying 6. act on their curiosity, take risks and be open to new ideas and uncertainty.

(NCCA 2009: 44)

Sample observation

Observation 2: Cognitive development

Date of observation: 1 November 2013

Time observation started and finished: 08.40–08.50

Number of children present: 1

Number of adults present: 1 staff member and 1 student (observer)

Permission obtained from: Supervisor

Description of setting: This observation took place in a registered childminder's home in a rural setting. While the childminder (and one co-worker) caters for children from six months to school-going age and also provides an after-school service, there are currently only one baby, two preschoolers and four after-school children attending. The facility is open from 8 a.m. to 6 p.m., Monday to Friday.

Immediate context: This observation took place in the playroom. It is a bright and airy room with a good variety of colourful toys available for the children. The observation took place at 8.40 in the morning. TC is the only child in and has been there from 8.00, as his mother goes to work early. At the time of the observation, the childcare worker is sitting down on the floor sorting out jigsaw puzzles that have become mixed up while chatting with TC. TC is sitting down playing with five small world figures: two Action Men (one dressed as an astronaut and one as an army man), Gangrene (Action Man's arch rival) and two figures from *Lord of the Rings*, Gandalf and Frodo. At the start of the observation, TC is holding one Action Man figure (the astronaut) and Gangrene in his hands and has the rest at his feet.

Brief description of the child observed: TC is a male aged three years and one month. He has been with this childminder since he was six months old and is very used to the place, treating it like home. TC has two older brothers (aged 12 and eight) and one older sister (aged six). He is a very active, talkative child.

Aim of observation: The aim of this observation is to observe TC for a period of 10 minutes in order to assess his cognitive development.

Rationale: It is important to observe children in order to plan developmentally appropriate activities for them.

Method: Narrative

Media used: Pen, refill pad

Observation

TC is sitting on the floor with his two legs out in front of him holding a naked Action Man figure in his right hand and Gangrene in his left (earlier TC removed Action Man's space suit). He uses his whole hand to grasp the figures, as they are quite large. He is bashing one off the other as if they are fighting. TC appears to be giving a running commentary on the fight, saying, 'Gangrene, huh ah, Gangrene.' Adult says to TC, 'Ah, don't hit Gangrene.'

TC says, 'Is that, what, will you put this on him?' (Referring to silver astronaut suit.) Adult says, 'Yes, we can't have him going round with nothing on him,' but does not put the clothes on him — she continues sorting the jigsaw puzzles. TC repeats — holding the suit out to adult — 'Put this on him.' Adult says, 'You put Action Man's trousers on him.' TC holds out the suit again and says, 'I can't put this on him. This big style costume, this big one, I've got my suit on me.' (Seems to be referring to self.) Adult says 'Yeah' and continues to sort jigsaws. TC bashes the action figures off each other again, saying, 'Oh buah, buah, buah, Gangrene, buah.' He asks again, 'Will you put his suit on him?' TC appears to be looking round for more clothes. Adult says, 'Will you help tidy?' TC says 'yeah' but makes no attempt to move. He begins to try to put on the action figure's suit. TC says again, 'Will you put this special suit on him?' When adult does not respond, TC says loudly, 'Do it, do it, do it . . . please.' (Seems to be getting frustrated.) The adult puts the suit on the action figure and hands it back to TC.

TC raises Gangrene and the Action Man with the space suit on him into the air over his head. He says, 'Gangrene can fly, whoosh, he can fly.' Adult says, 'Can he?' TC continues to play with action figures over his head, whooshing them over and back saying, 'De de ne, de de ne.' After a few seconds of doing this, TC drops the Action Man in the space suit and picks up the army Action Man and begins hitting him off Gangrene, again saying, 'Dah, dah.' He then begins walking around the room with the action figures still over his head, hitting them off each other and saying, 'Dah, dah, ooh.'

Adult asks TC, 'Which of them is your favourite?' TC says, 'This one.' (Appears to be looking at army Action Man in left hand.) Adult asks, 'Which one?' TC says, 'This one.' (Appears to be looking again at army Action Man in left hand.) Adult says, 'The one in your left hand?' TC answers, 'Yeah.' Adult asks, 'Don't you like him?' (Referring to Gangrene.) TC says, 'No, he's bad.' Adult asks, 'Who is the other fellow in the silver suit?' TC replies, 'Superman, Superman!' (There is no Superman figure present.) Adult asks, 'So you prefer Superman to Action Man?' TC laughs and says, 'No, that's Superman and that's Superman.' (Referring to the two Action Man figures.) Adult says, 'Oh, right.'

TC jumps up and down, saying, 'De ne de ne de ne de.' TC goes quickly down on all fours on the ground and begins bashing the two action figures off each other again. TC says, 'Got you, got you, got you, Gangrene.' TC then drops the army Action Man and begins to twist Gangrene's arm (when you do this, Gangrene's head swivels — one side of the head is a smiling Gangrene and the other is ugly). TC swivels to the ugly side, saying, 'Gangrene yuck, Gangrene yuck.'

TC now picks up one of two *Lord of the Rings* characters lying on the floor and says, 'That's *Lord of the Rings*.' Adult appears to look towards TC and asks, 'What do you call that fella?' TC says, 'Gandalf.' TC examines Gandalf's white hair closely, saying, 'White man, he's a white man.' TC then removes Gandalf's hat using a pincer grasp, saying while he is doing so, 'Take off that hat.' TC then picks up Frodo (another *Lord of the Rings* character) with his right hand and begins to take off his top. While he is doing this, TC says, 'I'm going to take off their clothes.' Adult says, 'Will they not be cold?' TC says, 'No.' Adult says, 'Oh, I would say they might be cold.' TC says, 'No, they are fighting mans, they are fighting mans,' and continues to remove their clothes, saying, 'Now they are in their bare buff.' Adult laughs and says, 'Wrestlers, are they?' TC says, 'Yeah, in his bare buff a wrestler.' TC then drops Frodo and picks up Gandalf again, saying, 'Gandalf, put your hat on.' TC puts Gandalf's hat on. TC then drops Gandalf and begins to get up, saying, 'Go outside, can I go outside?' TC runs towards adult, adult catches TC and begins tickling him. TC laughs. Adult says, 'Ah, TC's a great boy, isn't he?' TC laughs.

Observation ends

Evaluation (See Chapter 4, p. 93 for a note on the structure of evaluations.)

The aim of this observation was to observe TC, a three-year-old boy, for 10 minutes while at free play in order to gain a better understanding of his cognitive development. I feel that I achieved this aim very well as I am satisfied that I observed TC very closely and recorded everything he said and did accurately. I found that generally TC's cognitive development appears to be within the normal range for his age.

Cognitive development includes the development of imagination, creativity, memory skills, concentration skills, problem-solving skills and concept formation (Flood 2013). Some of these were evident in this observation. For much of the observation, TC used his imagination to act out or role play the battle between Action Man and Gangrene, his arch rival. This observation illustrates Bandura's point (1977) about how children copy or reflect what they see, especially if it is violent. TC has two older brothers and it is therefore likely that he has seen the Action Man cartoons on TV, where Action Man and Gangrene do battle with each other.

TC's memory skills are in evidence in that he can remember the names of all the characters, i.e. Gangrene, Frodo and Gandalf. TC also shows good concentration skills in that he stayed at the same activity over the 10 minutes and concentrated well when removing and putting on the action figures' clothes. TC was able to remove the astronaut's clothes but was not able to put them back on again. He made several attempts, but then realised that he could not succeed. He then asked the adult to help. This exchange was very interesting. The adult was preoccupied with sorting the jigsaws and was not really listening to TC. TC therefore had to solve the problem of getting the adult's attention so that she would put on the astronaut's suit. He tried to do this by changing the wording of his request each time. TC said, 'Will you put this on him', 'I can't put this on him ... this big costume, this big one', 'Will you put this

special suit on him?' In the end, TC gets frustrated and says loudly, 'Do it, do it, do it …
please.' He quickly says please because he seems to realise that he has been a bit forceful with
his request. He shows that he understands you have to be persistent with adults, but not too
demanding.

TC appears to have a good grasp of a number of different concepts. Gangrene is always the
action figure on the receiving end of things, which indicates that TC understands the concept
of good guy and evil villain. Also, when the adult asked him which figure he preferred, he
chose Action Man, also indicating that he doesn't like Gangrene because he is bad. This
indicates that TC understands that the villain is generally disliked.

TC also demonstrated that he knew what the concept 'wrestler' meant (a man stripped to
the waist who fights), even though he could not think of the name. Vygotsky's concept of
scaffolding was in evidence here in that the adult supplied the word 'wrestler', which TC used
in the next sentence when he said, 'Yeah, in his bare buff, a wrestler.' TC's use of the words
'bare buff' again demonstrates how he listens to and copies other people.

Piaget's idea of animism, where children actually believe inanimate objects have feelings,
may be in evidence in the observation in that TC acted as if there really was a fight going on
between Action Man and Gangrene.

Piaget believed that children under the age of four are not capable of seeing something
from another's perspective, that they are not capable of imagining what another person is
thinking, believing that everyone sees and thinks the same as they do. In this observation, the
adult asks TC if the action figure (in his hand) is Action Man. TC seems to know that the adult
already knows the answer to this question. Instead of answering, 'Yes, it is Action Man,' TC
decides to play a trick and says instead, 'Superman and Superman,' laughing as he does so. It
would seem as if TC knows that the adult knows it is Action Man, but is asking anyway.

While playing with Gandalf's hair (which is white), TC refers to Gandalf as 'white man, he's
a white man'. TC seems to be able to recognise the colour white. Children begin to be able to
name some colours from three years (Sheridan 1997).

In summary, TC's cognitive development in terms of imagination, memory, concentration,
problem solving and concept formation seems to be within the normal range for his age. The
observation in particular demonstrated how children learn by copying what they see.

Personal learning gained

- I learned a good deal more about children's cognitive development by observing
  imagination, memory, concentration, problem solving and concept formation. I observed
  how children can often understand a concept, e.g. wrestler, without having a name for it.

- I learned more about Piaget's pre-operational stage of development, but like many others, I question his finding that children under four are incapable of understanding a perspective other than their own.
- I saw the importance of Vygotsky's scaffolding in helping children in terms of cognitive and language development.

Recommendations

- I recommend that adults should engage with children in conversations in order to fully support their learning.
- Perhaps this child should have less exposure to cartoons or films with a violent content.

References

Flood, E. (2013), *Child Development for Students in Ireland* (2nd edn.). Dublin, Gill & Macmillan.

Sheridan, M., revised and updated by Sharma, A. and Cockerill, H. (1997), *From Birth to Five Years*, (3rd edn.). UK: Routledge.

Signatures

Sylvia Dolan   Date: 7/11/2013
Student

Joanne Lanney   Date: 20/10/2013
Supervisor

Jessica Smith   Date: 3/11/2013
Tutor

Revision questions

1. What six elements make up cognitive development?
2. What is symbolic play and why should it be encouraged in children?
3. What is role play and why should it be encouraged in children?
4. Define the term 'creativity'. Suggests ways in which children can be encouraged to express their creativity.
5. What three tasks are involved in memory?
6. What is childhood amnesia?
7. Suggest ways in which childcare workers can help children develop their memory skills.
8. Why is the development of concentration skills important?
9. Suggest ways in which childcare workers can help children develop their concentration skills.
10. Describe attention deficit and hyperactivity disorder. What problems can the disorder pose for the child?
11. Describe how children's approach to problem solving changes as they get older.
12. How do behaviourists believe children learn?
13. In Piagetian theory, what do the following terms mean: (a) schema (b) assimilation (c) accommodation (d) organisation (e) equilibrium and disequilibrium?
14. Describe Piaget's (a) sensori-motor and (b) pre-operational stages of development.
15. Piaget believed that children under four years are egocentric. What did he mean by this?
16. What is animism?
17. Piaget believed that children under seven years cannot conserve. What did he mean by this?
18. Describe two main criticisms of Piaget's theories.
19. What did Vygotsky mean by the zone of proximal development?
20. What is scaffolding in relation to children's cognitive development?
21. List six ways in which childcare workers can promote cognitive development in children.
22. Which Aistear theme is most closely linked to cognitive development?

Language Development

The structure of language

Language is any form of communication, be it spoken, written or signed. Language consists of words and a system of combining them. All human languages have five rules that organise and order them: phonology, morphology, syntax, semantics and pragmatics.

Phonology

Phonology is the sound system of a language. A phoneme is a basic unit of sound, e.g. 'ba'. Different languages have different phonemes. This is why, for example, many people from Pakistan have difficulty with the phoneme 'v' when speaking in English, as in the word 'very', since 'v' does not exist in Punjabi, the most commonly spoken language in Pakistan.

Morphology

Morphemes are the units that make up words. Sometimes words contain only one morpheme, e.g. 'rag', whereas sometimes they contain more than one, e.g. 'ragged' contains two. The grammar of a language depends on morphology. For example, 'he walks' and 'he walked' have two different meanings because of the morphemes added at the ends, 's' in one case and 'ed' in the other.

Syntax

Syntax is the way that words are combined in sentences to make understandable phrases. The same words combined differently can completely change the meaning of a phrase, e.g. 'John hit Peter' or 'Peter hit John'.

Semantics

Semantics refers to the meaning of words and sentences. Every word has a set of semantic features related to its meaning. Some words are close semantically, e.g. man and boy are close, whereas others are semantically very different, e.g. chair and dog (the only common semantic feature would perhaps be that they both have four legs). For sentences to make sense, the semantics have to be right. For example, while 'the horse spoke quietly to the boy' is grammatically correct, it is not semantically correct in that speaking is not a semantic feature associated with horses.

Pragmatics

Pragmatics involves knowing how to use language appropriately in different contexts. Compare the way you would use language in an interview with how you would use it while talking to your friends over a cup of coffee. Pragmatics is closely linked to a child's social development (see Chapter 7) and learning what is appropriate in given situations. For example, a young child displays their lack of understanding of pragmatics when they declare loudly in church that they have to go poo.

Overview of language development

The task of learning language is an extremely complex one, making it all the more remarkable that babies normally utter their first word by 13 months and by four years of age have mastered speech to an almost adult-like level. In order to learn even their first word, children must:

- Identify a word from a speech stream. (Think of how people speaking in a foreign language sound to you. Their speech seems to be just one long string of sounds with no gaps.)
- Remember what the word sounds like so they can recognise it again.
- Link the word with some consistent event, for example notice that every time the sound 'doggy' is said, a small furry creature appears.
- Physically train the vocal cords, tongue and lips to produce the correct sound.
- Say the word in an appropriate context.

The process of learning language begins at birth and infants the world over follow a similar pattern of development regardless of what language they learn.

Infancy

Long before babies speak recognisable words, they **vocalise**. There are several reasons for these early vocalisations, which include attracting attention, practising speech sounds and just for fun (babies love to experiment with their own voice). During the first year, babies' sounds go through a particular sequence.

- **Crying:** Babies cry from birth. Crying is initially used by babies only to signal distress (hungry, wind, dirty nappy, tired). Later, though, crying is used for a variety of reasons, e.g. pick me up, I am bored sitting here.
- **Cooing:** Babies first begin cooing between one and two months. Cooing is a gurgling sound made at the back of the throat and usually signals pleasure.
- **Babbling:** From about six months, babies begin stringing together speech-like sounds made up of a consonant and vowel – ba ba ba, da da da.

Infants begin to use gestures such as nodding or pointing between eight and 12 months. Children initially point without checking whether the adult is looking, but then they will point and look back to the adult to see if they are looking. No pointing is one of the early indicators of communication problems, e.g. autism.

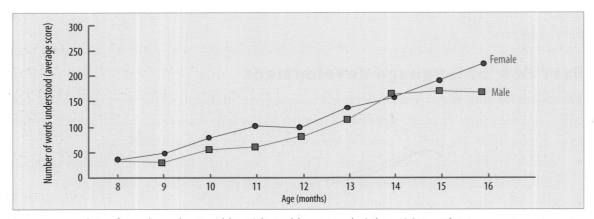

Average number of words understood by girls and boys aged eight to16 months

Infants understand many words before they can actually speak them. This is called their **passive or receptive vocabulary**. Some infants, for example, recognise their own name as early as five months. The graph above shows the average number of words understood by boys and girls aged eight to 16 months (Fenson et al. 1994: 74).

A child's first words usually include the names of familiar *people*, e.g. Nana, Dada, Mama; *objects*, e.g. ball; *animals*, e.g. doggy; *body parts*, e.g. eyes; *foods*, e.g. juice; and *greeting terms*, e.g. day-day. This is called their **active or spoken vocabulary**. As stated above, while there are wide variations among children as to when they speak their first words (nine to 24 months), on average, children utter their first words at around 13 months, speaking on average 20 to 50 words by 18 months. The graph below shows the average number of words spoken by boys and girls aged eight to 16 months (Fenson et al. 1994: 75).

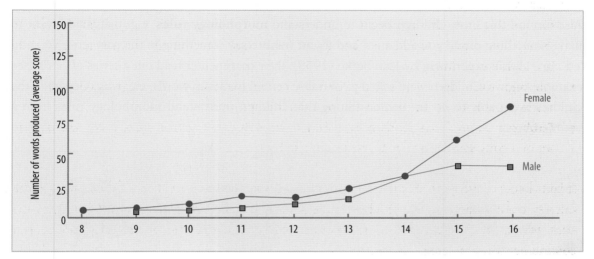

Average number of words spoken by girls and boys aged eight to16 months

Somewhere around 18 to 24 months (although again, this can vary considerably), children begin to rapidly produce new words (sometimes as many as 10 to 20 new words per week). This is called the **vocabulary spurt**. Another feature of language at this stage is the **over and under extension** of word meanings. For example, if a child has learned the word 'dada', they may apply this to all males (over extension). In contrast, if a child learns the word 'doggy' in relation to their own dog (a black and white border collie), they may not recognise that a golden retriever is also a dog (under extension).

Between 18 and 24 months, children usually begin to use two-word utterances such as 'mammy go', 'where daddy?', 'juice gone'. While these utterances are not full, grammatically correct sentences, they are remarkably understandable. This type of speech, where the usual grammatical structures of language are not adhered to, is called **telegraphic speech**.

Early childhood

From age two, toddlers move quickly from two-word utterances to creating three-, four- and five-word sentences. Sometimes children's understanding of the world around them is ahead of their speech. Take the three-year-old in the observation at the end of Chapter 5. While playing with two toy figurines, he began removing their tops. When the adult asked, 'Will they not be cold?', the boy replied, 'No they are fighting mans,' and began bashing them off each other. The three-year-old in this case had seen and understood the concept of wrestling but did not yet have the word for wrestler. Note also the three-year-old's incorrect use of the word 'mans'. This feature of children's speech will be dealt with later (see the section on Noam Chomsky, p. 130).

By age three, most children can pronounce all the **phonemes** (sounds) of their native language. Also around this time, children begin to understand **morphology rules**, e.g. that if you want to make something plural you add an 's' and if you want to say something in the past tense you add 'ed'. In a classic experiment by Jean Berko (1958), the experimenter read out a series of cards (see example below). Children were asked to pluralise certain made-up words, e.g. wug. Generally the children were able to do so, demonstrating that children understand morphology rules from a young age.

Wug experiment by Jean Berko

Another complex aspect of language is **syntax**, or word order, in a sentence. Consider these two sentences:

Where is Mammy going?
Mammy is going to work.

These seemingly simple sentences are actually very complex. To form them correctly, you have to know the differences in word order between question-type sentences and non-question-type sentences.

- Question-type sentence order: (1) 'wh' word ('Where') (2) auxiliary verb ('is') (3) subject ('Mammy') and (4) verb.
- Non-question-type sentence order: (1) subject ('Mammy') (2) auxiliary verb ('is') (3) verb ('going') (4) catenative verb ('to work').

Yet by and large, children master syntax by age four. One of the last aspects of syntax to be mastered is called the auxiliary inversion rule, whereby when you ask a question, 'is' comes before the subject of the sentence. This is why children may ask, 'Where Mammy is going?'

In terms of semantics (word understanding), it is estimated that between the ages of 18 months and six years, children learn on average one word for every hour they are awake, which totals approximately 14,000 words by age six (Clark 1993).

Early literacy

According to figures from the OECD, approximately 10 per cent of all Irish children have literacy problems, with the figure standing at over 30 per cent in areas designated as disadvantaged, so it is vital to understand how children's literacy skills develop or fail to develop. Literacy skills start with the development of language skills; as such, it is necessary that parents talk to their children about what their child is interested in. For example, if a child is playing with its teddy, then parents' talk should be about the teddy – 'Oh, teddy is lovely and soft, isn't he?' One study by Harris, Jones and Grant (1983) found that the mothers of children with language delay tended to speak less often to them, and that when they did speak, they often did not relate what they said to what the child was doing at the time.

Before learning to read, children begin describing and drawing things that are not physically there. This is called symbolic representation and is vital in the process of learning to read. The child must understand the concept that symbols can have meaning. Generally, there are two approaches to teaching children to read:
- The phonics approach.
- The whole-language approach.

The **phonics approach** emphasises the breakdown of words into their component parts and learning to 'translate' letter symbols into sounds. It is only after the child has mastered this that they progress to reading stories and poems.

In contrast, the **whole-language approach** is recommended by psychologists such as John Holt (1983), who believe that the phonics approach destroys the child's love of reading and takes away their natural ability to puzzle things out for themselves, just as they did while learning to speak. Holt recommends the use of real, interesting books for children even if they cannot read them from cover to cover.

Which approach is best is open to debate. Some studies show that the whole-language approach works best for children who are exposed to books at home, whereas children who have little exposure to books at home may get little practice outside school and may require the more direct phonics approach (Pressley 2007).

Many children who come from homes where reading is a daily activity come to school already reading, or at least possessing many of the prerequisites for reading – knowing that reading progresses from left to right, identifying letters of the alphabet and perhaps knowing how to write their own names. Others come from homes where there is little reading done or little access to reading materials. These children start school at a distinct disadvantage and frequently fall behind in the first two years, with many remaining behind for the rest of their schooling.

READING RECOVERY

Reading Recovery is an early intervention programme developed in New Zealand by the psychologist Marie Clay (1926–2007) for children who have made very little progress in reading and writing during their first year at school. It involves a daily one-to-one lesson with a highly trained teacher for a period of between 12 and 20 weeks. At the end of this time, most of these children have caught up with their classmates and can read and write at a level within the average band for their age. Reading Recovery has had huge success rates in many countries worldwide, including Ireland, by identifying and targeting children at risk of developing literacy difficulties before they begin to see themselves as poor readers. Once children begin to see themselves as poor readers they will then begin to avoid reading, thus perpetuating the problem.

Writing

Children's writing begins to emerge between the ages of two and three, when they start to draw and scribble. By age four, most children can write their own first name and by five most can print letters and copy short words. For the first few years of schooling, children with normal literacy abilities may reverse letters such as b and d, p and q. Like with reading, writing takes practice and children who are given frequent opportunities to write generally progress much more quickly. On page 129 is a child's note to her grandparents. She had called in to visit and, finding them not at home, left this correspondence letting them know she had called.

Example of a child's free writing, age six. This child is from an Irish border county. You can 'see' her Northern accent in the way she has written some of her words, e.g. 'to granddaddy we were here'.

Bilingualism and second language learning

How difficult is it to learn a second language? Can adolescents and adults learn a second language to fluency? Generally speaking, if a second language is learned before the age of 10 to 12, then the speaker will be more likely to achieve native-like pronunciation and accent, more accurate speech in terms of grammar and a more extensive vocabulary. This is why many people in Ireland would like to see the learning of a second European language during the primary school years (like many other countries) rather than beginning at secondary school, when the child has gone past the optimum age for language learning. There are many advantages to being bilingual other than just having a second language. Studies show that being able to speak more than one language has a positive effect on other aspects of cognitive development, such as attention, concept formation and reasoning (Gibbons and Ng 2004).

Theories of language development

Up to this point, this chapter has described patterns of language development. Now it is time to examine the theories that exist about *how* this development occurs. As with every other aspect of child development, the debate about whether language development occurs as a result of nature or nurture is to the forefront.

Nature (biological perspective)

Language certainly has biological origins. You could try to teach a cat to speak until the cows come home, but you would not succeed. Studies of brain-damaged patients have identified two main areas of the brain concerned with language – Broca's area (speech production and grammar) and Wernicke's area (language comprehension). Patients with damage to Broca's area have difficulty pronouncing words correctly, while patients with damage to Wernicke's area produce streams of correctly pronounced words that do not make sense.

Noam Chomsky (1928–)

The linguist Noam Chomsky has proposed that human beings are prewired to understand the complex grammatical structure of language. He believes that children are born with what he calls a **language acquisition device (LAD)** that enables them to detect rules and features of language such as morphology and syntax (described earlier). He believes that children's LAD begins to weaken with age, particularly between the ages of 10 and 12, and that native-like fluency after that age is virtually impossible. His findings have been supported by rare cases such as Genie (see below), where children who grow up in virtual isolation are unable to achieve fluency despite intensive language exposure when discovered.

One of Chomsky's key observations in support of his LAD theory is children's use of what he called **virtuous errors**. Very early on and all on their own, children seem to work out basic rules of grammar, such as adding 's' to pluralise a word and adding 'ed' to put a verb into the past tense. They then apply these rules even when they are not appropriate. Hence, children say things like 'I runned home as fast as I could' or 'My feets are dirty.' Chomsky contends that if English grammar (or indeed the grammar of other languages as well) followed its own rules, then these utterances would in fact be correct. Chomsky argues that environment could not be a factor here because children do not hear adults saying 'runned' and 'feets'.

THE STORY OF GENIE

Genie (not her real name) was a child who spent nearly all of the first 13 years of her life locked inside a bedroom strapped to a potty chair. She was a victim of one of the most severe cases of social isolation in history. Genie was discovered by American authorities on 4 November 1970 when her mother, who was almost completely blind, took her with her to claim disability benefits.

Genie was born in 1957, to a mother and father who were both mentally unstable. Genie had three older siblings, only one of whom survived, a brother. When Genie was between 14 and 20 months of age and just beginning to learn speech, a doctor told her family that she seemed to be developmentally delayed. Her father took the opinion more

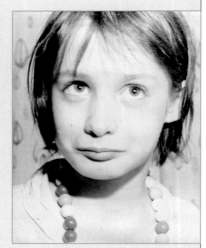

Genie

seriously than it was expressed by the doctor, apparently deciding that she was profoundly retarded, and subjected her to severe confinement and ritual ill treatment in an attempt to 'protect' her.

Genie spent the next 12 years of her life locked in her bedroom. During the day, she was tied to a child's potty chair, while at night, she was bound in a sleeping bag and placed in a cot which was covered over with wire mesh. It is believed that Genie's father beat her if she vocalised, and barked and growled at her like a dog in order to keep her quiet. He also rarely allowed his wife and son to leave the house or even to speak, and he absolutely forbade them to speak to Genie. By the age of 13, Genie was almost entirely mute, with a vocabulary of about 20 words and a few short phrases (nearly all negative), such as 'stop it' and 'no more'.

After Genie was discovered, she began a programme of extensive rehabilitation at Children's Hospital Los Angeles. On occasion, Genie lived with the psychologists working with her and also in a series of foster homes. Genie never learned to speak fluently and incorrectly constructed sentences, e.g. 'Applesauce buy store.' Her failure to master language completely is taken as evidence of Chomsky's theory that there is a critical age threshold for language acquisition. In 1984, Genie's mother successfully sued the Californian health authorities for their treatment of Genie, arguing that they treated Genie like a medical experiment and ignored her welfare as a human being. Genie is still alive today and lives in an undisclosed sheltered home in southern California for adults who cannot live independently. The film *Mocking Bird Don't Sing* was made in 2001 about the case.

Nurture (environmental perspective)

Behaviourist view

As discussed earlier in Chapter 5, behaviourists such as Skinner (1957) believe that learning, including language learning, occurs as a result of reinforcement. For example, if a baby accidentally babbles 'da da da' and Dada rewards this with smiles, hugs and saying 'good girl', in time the baby will repeat this behaviour intentionally to receive the positive reinforcement, in this way learning the word 'Dada'. It is widely accepted nowadays, however, that behaviourism alone cannot explain children's language development. Children are not reinforced for every word they learn, and why do virtuous errors occur?

Interactionist view

The **interactionist view**, while it does acknowledge the influence of biology, emphasises the importance of the child's social world in language learning. One of the most important aspects of a young child's linguistic environment is **child-directed speech** or **motherese**. Motherese is the name given to the natural way we speak to babies and young children. It is high pitched, uses simple words and short sentences. It usually relates to what the child is focusing his or her attention on at that moment in time. Other strategies automatically used by adults to help children's language development are recasting, expanding and labelling.

- **Recasting:** The adult tidies up what the child has said in a grammatically correct way. For example, if a child said, 'Mammy go home,' the adult may say, 'Yes, Mammy is going to go home now.'
- **Expanding:** The adult encourages the child to expand on what they have said. For example, the child says, 'Ice cream yum yum,' and the adult says, 'What colour ice cream is your favourite?'
- **Labelling:** Children constantly learn the names of things by pointing and asking. Adults patiently label items in their world for them.

The American psychologist **Jerome Bruner** (1915–) stresses the importance of the child's environment in language development. He believes that the adults and more able peers in a child's life provide what he calls a language acquisition support system (LASS). Motherese, recasting, expanding and labelling all form part of this system.

The key stages of language development

Age	Language development
1 month	Will stop whimpering to sound of soothing human voice or noise such as vacuum cleaner. Utters guttural throaty sounds when content. Coos. Cries loudly when hungry or uncomfortable.
3 months	Cries when hungry or uncomfortable. Will show excitement by kicking legs and waving arms at approach of carer. Vocalises delightedly when being played with.
6 months	Makes vowel sounds, e.g. goo, aaa, muh. Laughs, chuckles and screams in play. Can distinguish emotion in carer's voice, e.g. may cry if carer shouts. Note: Deaf babies will make vowel sounds.
9 months	Shouts to attract attention. Babbles tunefully, e.g. dad dad dad, mum, mum, mum. Responds to first name. Understands no and bye-bye. Understands where's teddy?, where's Daddy? by turning head to look. Deaf babies do not babble tunefully.
12 months	Babbles in a way that resembles speech. Understands simple instructions, e.g. give the doll to Mummy. Will imitate adult playful vocalisations, e.g. uh-oh! Uses pointing and will check if adult is looking.
15 months	Makes speech-like sounds. Usually says first two to six words and demonstrates by their actions that they understand many more. Will look at picture books for a few minutes at a time. Understands simple instructions, e.g. give Mammy the hairbrush. Points to familiar items or people when requested, e.g. where's Peter?, where's your belly? Extensive use of pointing to have needs met.

18 months	Chatters away to him/herself during play. Chattering will have many of the characteristics of real speech, e.g. raising and lowering of the tone of voice, etc. Responds to instructions and directions. Number of words used varies widely among different children, with some children, particularly girls, using as many as 100 recognisable words and understanding many more (Fenson et al. 1994). A vocabulary spurt often occurs at this time. Enjoys nursery rhymes and tries to sing. Will hand objects to carer even when a number of choices are available.
2 years	Vocabulary continues to expand and child may begin putting two words together to make sentences, e.g. Daddy go. Refers to self by name and talks in long incomprehensible monologues while at play. Echolalia (repetition of words) is present. Constantly pointing and asking the names of people and objects. Enjoys nursery rhymes and songs – will join in. Can follow two-step simple instructions, e.g. get your coat and look in the pocket.
2 ½ years	Uses 200 or more words. Sentence structure and pronunciation will be immature. Speech intelligible to familiars. Can say first and surname. Continues to imitate phrases (echolalia). Continually asks questions, e.g. Why? What? Who? Uses personal pronouns correctly – I, you, me. May stutter in eagerness to tell something. Will play with small world toys, talking about what is going on during the play, e.g. dolly is dirty, I wash dolly.
3 years	Large vocabulary. Speech is intelligible even to strangers. Still some immature pronunciation. Virtuous errors. Talks to self in long monologues about here and now only. Questioning continues. Can briefly describe past experiences. Begins to use descriptive language, e.g. the big wet dog jumped on me! Loves stories and asks for the same ones over and over. Can count to 10 by rote.
4 years	Speech is grammatically correct and completely intelligible. May show some immature sound substitutions, e.g. I want to wide my bike now. Questioning continues. Can listen to longer stories. Can count to 20 by rote. Loves nursery rhymes, jokes and songs. Can usually recognise letters of the alphabet. Understands that words move from left to right when reading. Will 'read' stories by looking at pictures.
5 years	Speech is fluent and in the main is grammatically correct. Loves stories. Can give full name, address, age and sometimes birthday. Asks the meaning of abstract words and tries to use them. Enjoys rhymes, poems, stories and jokes. Can tell stories back in sequence. Can read words with regular spelling. More able to read names of things, e.g. dog, cat, than words such as with, when.
6 years	Speech is fluent and grammatically correct. Continues to ask the meanings for words and will try to use them appropriately. Reading is progressing, with some children able to read simple story books independently. Can relate a story back in sequence but may concentrate on minor details rather than the bigger picture.

Language development in middle and late childhood (six to 12 years) (FETAC Level 6 only)

Children begin to use language increasingly to describe things or events that are not in the present. They begin to understand that the letters and combinations of letters of the alphabet represent the sounds of language. Children's vocabulary continues to increase from about 14,000 words at about age six to an average of 40,000 by age 11 or 12 (Santrock 2009). Children begin to make similar progress in grammar. They begin to understand and use comparatives (stronger, steeper, wider) and their understanding and use of complex sentence structures also increases, e.g. 'When the girl fell off the bicycle thankfully she was wearing a helmet.'

Children begin to use language in a more connected way, to form arguments, descriptions, definitions and narratives. They are able to do this orally before they can do so in writing, so classroom discussions are very important for this age group, with the teacher taking notes on the points being made for a later summary.

Children become increasingly interested in the meanings of words and should be encouraged to ask what they mean. Understanding of pragmatics (knowing when and where to use particular styles of language) also develops during the years six to 12, and by adolescence most teenagers have a good idea when particular styles of language are appropriate and when they are not, e.g. when to speak loudly and quietly.

While some children can read quite competently by age six to eight, reading is not generally used as a learning tool until later. This is because the effort of actually reading the material can be sufficient for the child without their having to understand complex content as well. Later, as reading becomes more automatic, children become able to read and comprehend what the author is saying at the same time.

Environmental factors – effects of family, society and culture on language development

Family

The issue of socio-economic status has been investigated in number of international studies. One large-scale American study conducted by Hart and Risley in 1995 found that professional parents spoke much more often to their zero-to-three-year-olds than did unemployed parents on welfare. While children in both types of family learned to talk, children of professional parents developed vocabularies twice as large as those with parents on welfare by the time they went to pre-school.

In a longitudinal study carried out by Dr Mariah Evans of the University of Nevada, it was found that the number of books in a child's home was a huge predictor of educational success. It was in fact an even stronger indicator than parental education levels. They found that while as few as 20 books can have an impact, the more books available to children on a wide variety of topics the better.

Social and cultural factors

The linguist Basil Bernstein (1924–2000), before obtaining his PhD, spent many years as a teacher in London. He was interested in the trend whereby working class children tended to do less well academically in language-based subjects when compared to their middle class counterparts, yet scored equally well in areas not requiring much language, such as mathematics. He began studying the language patterns of both groups and found that, in general, working class students used what he called the 'restricted code' in conversations, whereas the middle class students were more inclined to use the 'elaborated code'. The restricted code uses short, meaning-laden sentences and is suitable for insiders who share assumptions and understanding on the topic, e.g. 'He's some chancer'. The elaborated code on the other hand does not assume that the listener shares these assumptions or understandings, and thus the elaborated code is more explicit, more thorough, and does not require the listener to read between the lines, so that 'He's some chancer' would be expressed as something like 'He would try anything to make some money'. Bernstein did not feel that one code was necessarily superior to the other, but noted that to do well in examinations you had to be fluent in the elaborated code. Exam answers require you to be explicit and thorough, and so favour students who use this style of language in everyday life.

Bernstein's findings are very much linked to family factors dealt with above. Working class households tend to use the restricted code while speaking to each other, whereas in middle class homes the elaborated code is used much more commonly. It was found that middle class parents were much more inclined to engage in lengthier conversations and discussions with their children than were working class parents. In this way middle class children were being given opportunities to practise skills required for educational success on daily basis.

In America, during the 1960s, studies were conducted into language use by low-income African-American children. At the time African-American English was dismissed as not being a valid language and it was recommended that these children should be formally taught English. The American William Labov (1969), together with many other linguists since, have studied the social dialects of lower-income African-American children in pre-school and school settings both inside and outside the classroom (playground). They disagreed with the verbal-deficit theories of the 1960s, finding that black English is a separate language system with its own grammar and rules.

How a language is spoken, even when they speak the same language, such as English, varies between cultural groups and reflects a culture's shared history and experiences. The American linguist and anthropologist Edward Sapir (1884–1939) and his student Benjamin Whorf (1897–1941) believed that the way we think and view the world is strongly influenced by our language, and not the other way round. This idea has come to be known as the Sapir–Whorf hypothesis. Take how Irish people speak about the weather – even on a nice day our comments are always tinged with negativity, e.g. 'Lovely day today, but how long will it last?' The Sapir–Whorf hypothesis would contend that the way we think about something like the Irish weather is determined by how we speak about it.

Promotion of language development

There are many ways language development may be promoted, such as the following.

- Use plenty of child-directed speech (motherese) with babies and toddlers. This type of speech is most easily understood by infants.
- Turn-take – allow infants time to 'answer' when you are talking to them.
- When talking to babies and young toddlers, talk to them about what their attention is focused on at that particular point in time.
- Use picture books, rhymes and action songs with younger children.
- Listen to young children and give them time to say what it is they are trying to say. Do not interrupt or finish their sentences for them.
- Enhance children's language by recasting, expanding and labelling (see above).
- Read stories to children, particularly books that rhyme or are funny, e.g. Dr Seuss series.
- Build up a well stocked, well maintained library in the setting. It is ideal if the area is carpeted, away from noisy areas of the pre-school room and has comfortable seating.
- Older children may like to listen to tapes or CDs of their favourite books while reading them. This allows them to listen to interesting stories that they cannot read independently yet.
- Give children plenty of opportunity to practise writing, for instance, allow them write short shopping lists. Make sure to use the list they have worked hard to create.
- There is some excellent interactive computer software available that encourages reading, such Wordshark and Reading for Literacy.
- Parents and afterschool service personnel should allow time every evening to talk to children. Discuss their day with them. Older children should be encouraged to discuss their opinions on things that are happening in the world.
- Build a library visit into the family's weekly routine. This encourages children to read and assists language and cognitive development.

- Try to build up a good stock of interesting books at home. Books like *Guinness World Records* or *Ripley's Believe It or Not!* are very good for dipping in and out of.
- Supervise children's homework (at home or in afterschool clubs), challenging them to discover and use new words. Use the internet to assist with this.
- Some schools have set up blogs where children can post their writings. Sensitively help children to spellcheck and proofread their work before posting.

How Aistear promotes language development

While all of Aistear's four themes promote language development the theme **communicating** does so very directly. The table below shows what Aistear sets out to do in this area of the early years curriculum. Early years workers provide unstructured and structured play opportunities designed to fulfil these aims and learning goals.

Theme: Communicating	
Aims	**Learning goals**
Aim 1: Children will use non-verbal communication skills.	In partnership with the adult, children will: 1. use a range of body movements, facial expressions, and early vocalisations to show feelings and share information 2. understand and use non-verbal communication rules, such as turn-taking and making eye contact 3. interpret and respond to non-verbal communication by others 4. understand and respect that some people will rely on non-verbal communication as their main way of interacting with others 5. combine non-verbal and verbal communication to get their point across 6. express themselves creatively and imaginatively using non-verbal communication.
Aim 2: Children will use language.	In partnership with the adult, children will: 1. interact with other children and adults by listening, discussing and taking turns in conversation 2. explore sound, pattern, rhythm and repetition in language 3. use an expanding vocabulary of words and phrases, and show a growing understanding of syntax and meaning 4. use language with confidence and competence for giving and receiving information, asking questions, requesting, refusing, negotiating, problem-solving, imagining and recreating roles and situations, and clarifying thinking, ideas and feelings 5. become proficient users of at least one language and have an awareness and appreciation of other languages 6. be positive about their home language, and know that they can use different languages to communicate with different people and in different situations.

Theme: Communicating (continued)	
Aims	**Learning goals**
Aim 3: Children will broaden their understanding of the world by making sense of experiences through language.	In partnership with the adult, children will: 1. use language to interpret experiences, to solve problems, and to clarify thinking, ideas and feelings 2. use books and ICT for fun, to gain information and broaden their understanding of the world 3. build awareness of the variety of symbols (pictures, print, numbers) used to communicate, and understand that these can be read by others 4. become familiar with and use a variety of print in an enjoyable and meaningful way 5. have opportunities to use a variety of mark-making materials and implements in an enjoyable and meaningful way 6. develop counting skills, and a growing understanding of the meaning and use of numbers and mathematical language in an enjoyable and meaningful way.
Aim 4: Children will express themselves creatively and imaginatively.	In partnership with the adult, children will: 1. share their feelings, thoughts and ideas by story-telling, making art, moving to music, role-playing, problem-solving, and responding to these experiences 2. express themselves through the visual arts using skills such as cutting, drawing, gluing, sticking, painting, building, printing, sculpting, and sewing 3. listen to and respond to a variety of types of music, sing songs and make music using instruments 4. use language to imagine and recreate roles and experiences 5. respond to and create literacy experiences through story, poetry, song and drama 6. show confidence in trying out new things, taking risks, and thinking creatively.

(NCCA 2009: 35)

Sample observation

Observation 3: Language development

Date of observation: 15 November 2013

Time observation started and finished: 17.00–17.08

Number of children present: 2

Number of adults present: Parent and 1 student (observer)

Permission obtained from: Parent

Description of setting: This observation took place in the child's own home. The child's home is a detached house in a rural setting.

Immediate context: This observation took place in the kitchen. TC is seated at the kitchen table colouring a picture of *The Simpsons* cartoon characters. His mother is standing nearby, ironing. The observation took place at 5.00 in the evening three days after TC started school. TC's older brother is sitting on the floor nearby playing with Kinex.

Brief description of the child observed: TC is a male aged four years and five months old. He has been in a crèche since he was six months old and has now just recently gone to primary school. He has one older brother (aged seven). Because both children attend a small country school, they are both in the same room at primary school. He is a very active, talkative child.

Aim of observation: The aim of this observation is to observe TC for a period of eight minutes in order to assess his language development.

Rationale: It is important to observe children in order to plan developmentally appropriate activities for them.

Method: Pre-coded

Media used: Pen, refill pad

Observation	Key:
	A→TC (Adult speaks to target child) TC→A (Target child speaks to adult)
	C→A (Other child speaks to adult) M, N, O, P (Other children)

Code	Language
A→TC	Did you make any new friends at school?
TC→A	Yeah, M and N and I play with them at lunchtime.
A→TC	What sort of games do you play?
TC→A	Mm, we play tag and duck, duck, goose.
A→TC	What's duck, duck, goose?
TC→A	Ya have to say duck and whoever you say goose to they're on and they have to try and catch ya and if you don't run quickly then they'll dus catch ya. I runned the fastest.
C→A	And if you get into their place on time then they have to do duck, duck, goose.
A→TC	I see.
TC→A	Will I do this blue? (referring to shorts on Bart Simpson)
A→TC	Yes, his shorts are blue, good man. And what else did you do? What's the best thing?
TC→A	Eh, playing around at the yard.
A→TC	And was there anything good you did in the classroom?
TC→A	And we had to do a snake, I had to do little skirkles really tiny, I did them all big and messy. I thought you had to do them big.
A→TC	Did you?
TC→A	Yeah.
A→TC	Did the teacher say it was messy?
TC→A	Yeah.
C→A	Yeah, it was the messiest.
A→C	No, don't say that C.
TC→A	Yeah, she said she thought it was play school. (laughs)
A→TC	What?
TC→A	Play school.
A→TC	And what about your friends in small school, little school?
TC→A	O and P?
A→TC	And do you miss them?
TC→A	No.

A→TC	Why?
TC→A	Because they are going to my birthday, just ring up them.
A→TC	Yeah.
TC→A	Ring up them now.
A→TC	But sure, your birthday is not for a while.
TC→A	Tomorrow?
A→TC	No.
TC→A	When?
A→TC	Not till March, pet, not for a long time.
TC→A	Oh, can I go out now?
A→TC	Yes, out you go, good man.

Observation ends

Evaluation

(See Chapter 4, p. 93 for a note on the structure of evaluations.)

The aim of this observation was to observe and record the language of TC, an almost four-and-a-half-year-old boy, for eight minutes while he was sitting colouring a picture, in order to gain a better understanding of his language development. I feel that I achieved this aim very well because the conversation was taped and accurately transcribed. Generally TC's language development appears to be within the normal range for his age.

By and large, TC's word pronunciation is accurate. He does make some errors, e.g. he says 'skirkles' for 'circles'. Other mispronunciations are more as a result of his accent, e.g. 'ya' instead of 'you' and 'dus' instead of 'just', rather than as a result of an inability to pronounce the words correctly. This is usual for his stage of development. While children between four and five years pronounce most words correctly, they 'may show some immature sound substitutions' (Flood 2013).

Children by and large master syntax, i.e. word order, in sentences by age four (Flood 2013). In this case, TC has managed to master syntax in that he makes only one syntactic error, saying 'ring up them now' instead of 'ring them up now'. All of his other sentences, some of them quite complex, e.g. his account of how to play duck, duck, goose, are all syntactically correct.

One of Noam Chomsky's key observations in support of his language acquisition device theory is children's use of what he calls virtuous errors. He believes that all on their own and very early on, children work out basic rules of grammar, such as adding 's' to pluralise a word and adding 'ed' to put a verb into the past tense. They then apply these rules even when they are not appropriate. TC uses one virtuous error during this observation when he says 'I runned the fastest', thus supporting Chomsky's theory.

TC shows a good understanding of the meaning of language, i.e. semantics, even when the speaker's exact meaning is not completely obvious. TC understood what his teacher meant when she criticised the messiness of his snake by saying 'she said she thought it was playschool'. He does not seem to be too upset by this criticism (he laughed). This is perhaps because he realises that he merely misunderstood what the teacher wanted, i.e. small circles, and therefore does not feel bad about his messiness.

In summary, TC's language development in terms of pronunciation, syntax and semantics seems to be within the normal range for his age. This observation also supports Chomsky's theory of language development in that TC used one virtuous error.

Personal learning gained

- I learned a good deal more about children's language development. I now have a better understanding of the terms 'semantics' and 'syntax'.
- I learned more about Chomsky's theory of language development and have witnessed and recorded a child using a virtuous error.
- I have learned how difficult it is to accurately record speech and believe that in order to do so accurately, a tape recording with transcription is advisable.

Recommendations

- I recommend that this child's parents continue to make time after each school day to sit down and discuss what happened that day. As Hart and Risley (1995) found, children who are engaged every day in conversation at home have an increased vocabulary and tend to succeed better in school.
- I recommend that this child's parents use open-ended questions when speaking to him. This will encourage him to elaborate on his answers and not just give short restricted answers.

References

Flood, E. (2013), *Child Development for Students in Ireland* (2nd edn.). Dublin, Gill & Macmillan.

www.en.wikipedia.org/wiki/Noam_Chomsky

Signatures

Deirdre Walsh
Student

Date: <u>25/3/2013</u>

Joan Smith
Parent

Date: <u>25/3/2013</u>

Jessica Neagle
Tutor

Date: <u>22/2/2013</u>

Revision questions

1. What do the following terms mean in relation to language: (a) phonology (b) morphology (c) syntax (d) semantics (e) pragmatics?
2. Outline the tasks a baby must complete before it utters its first words.
3. What is the difference between passive/receptive and active/spoken vocabulary?
4. What is the vocabulary spurt and when does it normally occur?
5. What is meant by telegraphic speech?
6. What are morphology rules?
7. Why is an understanding of symbolic representation necessary before learning to read?
8. Describe the two principal approaches that can be taken to teach children to read.
9. What are the advantages of bilingualism? When should children begin learning a second or third language?
10. Outline Noam Chomsky's theory of language development.
11. What is child-directed speech or motherese?
12. Describe Jerome Bruner's language acquisition support system.
13. Describe two environmental factors that can affect language development in children.
14. Outline six ways children's language development can be promoted in the childcare setting.
15. Describe three ways language development can be promoted in the home.
16. How does Aistear promote language development?

CHAPTER SEVEN

Social Development

Chapter outline

- What is social development?
- Interacting effectively with others
- Bullying (FETAC Level 6 only)
- Understanding the norms of society
- Moral development
- Special needs that affect social skills
- Pro-social and antisocial behaviour in children
- Effective management of children's behaviour
- How Aistear promotes social development
- Sample observation
- Revision questions

What is social development?

Social development can be defined as:

- Developing an ability to interact effectively with others.
- Developing an understanding of the norms (ways) of the society in which you live.
- Developing a sense of right and wrong (moral development).

Interacting effectively with others

Infancy

Babies are predisposed to be social from birth. There is nothing like a new baby's cry to attract attention and the power of an infant's smile is like no other. As John Bowlby (1958) said, 'It is fortunate for their survival that babies are so designed by nature that they beguile and enslave mothers.' Two types of smile can be distinguished in infants: the reflexive and the social smile. The reflexive smile occurs during the first month after birth, usually during sleep, and is caused by some internal stimuli, e.g. wind, and not by the child's external environment. The social smile occurs as early as four to six weeks, becoming more frequent as the baby gets older, and is in response to a carer's voice and smiles. After six months, smiles are accompanied by the Duchenne marker (constricting or crinkling of the eyes).

Early childhood

While infants as young as six months take notice and sometimes show an interest in other babies, it is not until approximately 18 months to two years that toddlers begin interacting with peers, and even then, **parallel play** still predominates, whereby the toddler will play happily alongside peers but not with them. By two and a half, toddlers engage in sustained role play, and after watching other children at play with interest may join in for a few minutes. By three years, the toddler understands what it is to share and joins in make-believe play with other children. By four years, the child will understand turn taking as well as sharing and will co-operate with peers. By this age, the child seeks out the companionship of others and will alternate between playing and fighting with peers. Also by four, the child understands that arguments, e.g. over a toy, need to be sorted out verbally and not by physically fighting. By five years, children understand the need for rules and fair play and they begin to choose their own friends.

Playing board games promotes co-operative play

Middle to late childhood (FETAC Level 6 only)

As children get older (beyond about age six) they begin to notice difference and start to compare themselves with others. Children begin to seek out friendships and friendship groups. As children get older co-operative play dominates, whereby children predominantly play as part of a group. Peer statuses begin to emerge within groups – group leaders and followers. This is a time when unfortunately some children, for various reasons, can become isolated or rejected by their peer groups (see **Peer relationships** below). It is also a time when bullying can occur among children.

Bullying

Bullying is a behavioural problem which affects the lives of thousands of Irish school children and their families. A nationwide study of bullying in Irish schools indicates that approximately 31 per cent of primary students and 16 per cent of secondary students have been bullied at some time; this equates to approximately 200,000 students (O'Moore 1997). Children who are bullied often experience fear, humiliation, social isolation and loss of self esteem. Children who are bullied often avoid going to school, so that their school work suffers. Bullying can cause personality change, illness, depression and unfortunately sometimes suicide.

Types of bullying behaviour

Verbal bullying occurs when children are called names, verbally insulted or made fun of. Sometimes a child's family, culture, race or religion is insulted. Spreading of malicious rumours is a particularly hurtful form of verbal bullying.

Physical bullying occurs when children are physically pushed, punched, pinched, kicked or hurt in other ways. While both boys and girls engage in physical bullying, it more commonly occurs among boys and is more likely to be classified incorrectly as horseplay.

Gesture bullying occurs when a child use gestures, such as staring, to intimidate another child.

Exclusion bullying occurs when a child is deliberately excluded from a group. This form of bullying causes tremendous damage to a child's self-esteem as it makes them feel that nobody likes them.

Extortion bullying occurs when children are threatened and demands are made to hand over items such as money or possessions.

E-bullying occurs when the bully uses technology to bully and intimidate. Social networking sites, texts and emails can all be used to spread vicious rumours, abuse and intimidate. This form of bullying is particularly difficult for the victim to deal with as it can be difficult to escape from; even at home the bully can make contact.

Causes of bullying

Why do some children bully?

While each case is different, children are more likely to be bullies if they:

- Are exposed to violence at home, e.g. witnessing domestic violence, being subject to harsh punishments.
- Are permitted to view violence, for instance on video games or television.
- Experience poor, inconsistent parenting.
- Are constantly criticised at home.
- Witness violent verbal outbursts by adults at home.
- Are given too much freedom and not enough discipline.
- Witness other domestic problems such as parental drug or alcohol abuse.

Bullying is more likely to be a problem in schools if:

- Rules are inconsistent or erratically enforced.
- Children are inadequately supervised.
- Staff do not treat children with respect, for instance using sarcasm or put-downs as punishment.
- An inadequate anti-bullying programme, policy and procedures are in place.

Why are some children bullied?

Despite the stereotypical images, any child can be bullied. Most bullying happens initially for no identifiable reason. Often the victim was just in the wrong place at the wrong time. Anything, even something very small, may be enough to set the victim apart as 'different' from the bully and in this way set them up as a target. For instance, a child who is a good reader may be bullied by a child with literacy issues. When children are bullied over a long period of time they begin to lose confidence and may begin to believe what the bullies are saying, blaming themselves for the bullying. This has a hugely detrimental effect on self-esteem and self-image.

Researchers have identified a group of children sometimes called 'provocative victims'. These children, perhaps due to lack of social skills or a learning difficulty, behave in ways that cause irritation or tension around them, making them vulnerable to bullying.

Where does bullying take place?

Bullying can occur almost anywhere, but particularly where there is either inadequate or no adult supervision. O'Moore (1997) found that in Irish primary schools, 74 per cent of children who said they were bullied reported that they were bullied in the playground, and 31 per cent in the classroom. Second level students reported the classroom to be the most common place to be bullied (47 per cent), with corridors (37 per cent) and playgrounds (27 per cent) also likely areas. Other reported areas included toilets, changing rooms, locker areas and dormitories in boarding schools. Nineteen per cent of primary school children who said they were bullied said that the incidents occurred going to or from school, while 8.8 per cent of second level students said the same. This study, carried out in 1997, makes no mention of cyber-bullying, which of course can invade all areas of a child's life, even their own bedroom.

Signs that a child may be being bullied

- Unexplained bruising, cuts or damage to clothing.
- Child shows signs of anxiety or distress – refuses to say what is wrong.
- Unexplained mood swings or behaviour:
  - becoming withdrawn
  - becoming clingy
  - attention-seeking
  - aggressive behaviour.
- Out-of-character behaviour in class.
- Deterioration in educational attainments.
- Loss of concentration.
- Loss of interest in school.
- Skipping school or complaining of illness to avoid school.
- Lingering behind in school after classes are over.
- Increased requests for pocket money, or stealing money.
- Loss of or damage to personal possessions or equipment.
- Artwork expressing inner turmoil.

(From Anti-bullying Centre website, TCD: www.abc.tcd.ie/school.html)

What can schools and parents do?

Parents	Schools
• Discuss the issue of bullying with your children. • Challenge every incident of bullying you witness or hear about, e.g. if your child describes to you how a child was treated badly that day. • Encourage your child to report incidents. • Be aware of your own behaviour. • Support your child's school in their efforts to combat bullying. • Give children advice about what to do if they are being bullied.	• Raise awareness of bullying, e.g. through anti-bullying workshops. • Have a clear anti-bullying policy. • Implement preventative measures, e.g. proper supervision at lunchtime, challenging 'slagging' and other potentially bullying behaviours. • Teach children how to deal effectively with conflict. • Be vigilant. • Advise parents of children being subjected to cyber-bullying to print material and report it to the school immediately. • Parents may be advised to report cyber-bullying to the gardaí.

Helping children combat bullying – advise children to:

- Tell someone they trust – their parents, teachers, friends. Stress that telling will not make the situation worse.
- Act as confidently as they can, make eye contact and clearly tell the bully to stop. Move away.
- Don't hit out – tell the child that they may get hurt or the bully may claim that they are the victim.
- If children are being called names, tell them to try not to show they are annoyed: bullies are looking for this reaction.
- Reassure the child that it is the bully that has the problem, not them.
- Tell them not to believe anything the bully says; it is not true.

Relationships during childhood

Sibling relationships

Over 80 per cent of children born in Ireland have one or more siblings. Sibling relationships can be very important in developing social skills such as helping, sharing, teaching and conflict resolution. Judy Dunn (2007) found that sibling relationships showed three main characteristics: the expression of intensive positive and negative emotions; siblings tended to alternate between being highly supportive of each other to teasing and undermining each other; and siblings tended to describe each other in either warm and affectionate ways or as being irritating and mean.

When siblings fight, parents tend to deal with it in one of three ways: intervene and help siblings sort out differences; give out and threaten; or do nothing and let them sort it out themselves. In terms of learning social skills, the first strategy is considered best, as it allows children to practise the skills needed to effectively resolve conflict situations in a calm and respectful manner (Kramer and Radley 1997).

What about only children? Contrary to popular belief, only children do not turn out to be self-centred and spoiled; research shows that they tend instead to be achievement orientated and display many positive personality traits. When only children first attend preschool or school, they frequently have a lot of ground to make up in terms of social development, but most manage to do so and there is no research to show that only children are less socially able than children with siblings.

Peer relationships

From about four years, children begin to observe their peers with interest and compare themselves to them. They begin to try to work out how to integrate themselves smoothly into peer activities and begin friendships with selected peers. Longitudinal research has shown that success at forming peer relationships is very important for later development. Children who have difficulty making friends often have difficulty later in life with relationships, reduced work success and mental health problems (Collins and van Dulmen 2006).

Three social skills are particularly important in forming successful peer relations: perspective taking, social information processing and emotional regulation.

- **Perspective taking:** This involves the child being able to consider a situation from another's point of view. This skill is very important for successful peer relations. According to Piaget (see Chapter 5), children have difficulty with this until about the age of four and tend to see things only from their own perspective. Adults should encourage the development of this skill in children by asking children things like, 'How do you think Josh felt when you pushed him over like that?'

- **Social information processing:** This involves the child accurately interpreting what is going on in a given situation and acting appropriately. For example, two children, Peter and Keith, are playing in the playground. Peter, who is big for his age, accidentally bumps into Keith and knocks him over. If Keith is good at processing social information, then he will interpret the situation as being accidental and tell Peter it is OK. On the other hand, if Keith is poor at processing social information, then he could react aggressively or go in to tell the teacher. Children who repeatedly misinterpret social information like this often have difficulty with peer relations and become unpopular.
- **Emotional regulation:** This involves the child being able to control their emotions, particularly anger and aggression. Likewise, children, particularly boys, who cry a lot often have difficulty forming peer relationships.

These three factors are seen to be important in determining a child's peer status. Wentzel and Asher (1995) interviewed large groups of school children, asking them who in their class group they liked most and least. They found that children can be divided into five different peer status groups.

- **Popular children:** These children have mastered the three social skills above and are frequently nominated as a best friend and rarely disliked by peers. Popular children usually listen to others, have a positive, happy disposition, control their negative emotions, show concern for others and are self-confident.
- **Average children:** These children receive an average number of both positive and negative nominations from their peers.
- **Neglected children:** These children do not receive many nominations, either positive or negative, from their peers. These children are usually very shy.
- **Rejected children:** These children are not often nominated as someone's best friend, but are frequently nominated as someone who is disliked. Generally they have not mastered any of the three social skills mentioned above and are often aggressive and troublesome.
- **Controversial children:** These children are frequently nominated as a best friend, but also as someone who is disliked.

Understanding the norms of society

Social norms are descriptions or 'rules' about people's behaviour, beliefs, attitudes and values within a society or social group. Blowing your nose into a tissue or being quiet while in a library are both examples of social norms. Social norms can vary subtly between social groups within society and in different social situations. For example, regarding the former, the use of bad language in everyday speech is socially acceptable within some groups in society, whereas within others it is frowned upon as being crude and uneducated. Regarding the latter, for example, children may curse in the playground but not in the classroom. Social norms are not legal rules, but the penalty for not obeying them may be social exclusion, depending on how important the social norm is. Children generally learn social norms through experience and there are two broad theories about how they learn from experience: the behaviourist view and the social modelling or social learning theory.

Behaviourist view

The behaviourist view, influenced predominately by the work of B.F. Skinner (1904–90), is that children learn as a result of reinforcement (see also Chapter 5). Reinforcement can be either negative (punishments) or positive (rewards). Behaviourists believe that positive reinforcements are much stronger and more effective learning tools than negative. From very early on, parents and other people around children begin the process of teaching them social norms. For example, if a two-year-old child begins picking their nose, they will be told, 'No, no, no – we must use a tissue,' and is then given a tissue to use. If the child begins using the tissue even very ineffectually, they will be praised: 'Yes, good boy, using his tissue.'

Social modelling or social learning theory

Social modelling or social learning theory is predominantly the work of the psychologist Albert Bandura (1925–). Basically, social learning theory proposes that people learn through observing others' behaviour and attitudes and the outcomes of those behaviours and attitudes. This is why it is vital that children are exposed to good role models from early on and why behaviours and attitudes learned in childhood through social modelling are so difficult to change. Take this example: a child is being told at school that they should keep their litter until they find a bin and dispose of it there. While the same child is being driven home from school by a parent, he or she witnesses the parent throwing litter from their car window. Is this child likely to litter or not?

Moral development

Moral development involves changes to how people think, feel and behave regarding standards of right and wrong. There are four different aspects to moral development, each of which will be dealt with in turn below.

- **Moral thought:** Changes to how the individual thinks about morally demanding questions.
- **Moral behaviour:** Changes to how the individual acts in morally demanding situations.
- **Moral feeling:** Changes to how the individual feels in morally demanding situations.
- **Moral personality:** The role of personality in moral development.

(1) Moral thought

Two psychologists who concerned themselves with how moral thought develops in children were Jean Piaget (1932) and Lawrence Kohlberg (1958). Both psychologists were similar in that they both believed that moral thought occurs in a series of stages.

Piaget

Piaget developed his theory of children's moral development by interviewing and observing them at play. He asked them questions about ethical issues such as telling lies, stealing, punishment and justice. Piaget found that children go through two distinct stages in their moral development with a period of transition in between.

- **Heteronomous morality (up to age seven):** During this stage, children see morality in a very black and white manner. They see rules and regulations as being fixed and unchangeable, handed down from on high, e.g. the teacher. Whether they will or will not be punished for some wrongdoing will be the main focus. At this stage, children do not take into account the intentions of another person when an act of wrongdoing has been committed. For example, Sandra is accidentally knocked over by Ken in the school yard. If Sandra is at this stage of moral development, she will not consider whether Ken meant to knock her over. She will feel that Ken should be punished for knocking her over because teacher says you should be careful not to knock people over in the yard. This is called **immanent justice,** a belief that misdeeds are automatically connected to punishments. Immanent justice also leads to the belief that if something unfortunate happens to an individual, that this is punishment for some earlier misdeed, e.g. if Ken subsequently falls in the yard, Sandra will think of this as punishment for having knocked her over. It is because of this link between misdeed and consequence that children are so preoccupied with punishment, frequently telling on each other even for small incidents, e.g. 'Teacher, Joan is after writing in pen in her maths copy instead of pencil.' Children at this age generally cannot tell lies about whether they carried out a misdeed or not. This is because they have not yet developed the understanding that if a misdeed is not witnessed, only they know what they did. Because of egocentric thinking (see Chapter 5), they think everybody else knows what they know.
- **Transition phase (seven to 10 years):** During this stage, children show some features of both stages.
- **Autonomous morality:** Children during this stage become aware that rules and regulations are created by people and that they are there to be negotiated. When children are judging and acting at this stage, they are capable of taking the intentions of the 'wrongdoer' into account. Using the example above, Sandra would get up and dust herself off, saying, 'It's OK, Ken, I know it was an accident.' After the age of seven, as outlined in Chapter 5, children are able to

decentre, i.e. see things from more than one point of view or perspective, which also enables children to lie. They begin to realise that they can possess information that other people do not have. In the beginning, some children lie even when all the evidence is against them, e.g. a child lying about eating chocolate cake even though it is all over their face. Later, children can weigh up the evidence to determine if a lie is believable or not. Some children, however, even if they are cognitively able to lie choose not to. These children tend to come from households and schools where parents and teachers discuss wrongdoing with the children and involve the children in dealing with it.

Kohlberg

Kohlberg (1927–87), like Piaget, believed that children pass through a series of stages during moral development. Piaget, as you have seen above, believed there were two main stages with a transition period in between. Kohlberg believed there were three distinctive levels, each of which had two sub-stages. Kohlberg gathered the data for his stage theory by presenting children of different ages with moral dilemmas followed by a series of questions. Kohlberg then categorised the children's answers. Here is an example of one of Kohlberg's dilemmas.

DILEMMA

Two young men who were brothers had got into serious trouble. They were secretly leaving town in a hurry and needed money. Karl, the older one, broke into a store and stole a thousand dollars. Bob, the younger one, went to a retired old man who was known to help people in town. He told the man that he was very sick and that he needed a thousand dollars to pay for an operation. Bob asked the old man to lend him the money and promised that he would pay him back when he recovered. Bob wasn't really sick at all, and he had no intention of paying the man back. Although the old man didn't know Bob very well, he lent him the money. So Bob and Karl skipped town, each with a thousand dollars.

1. (a) Which is worse, stealing like Karl or cheating like Bob?
    (b) Why is that worse?
2. (a) What do you think is the worst thing about cheating the old man?
    (b) Why is that the worst thing?
3. In general, why should a promise be kept?
4. (a) Is it important to keep a promise to someone you don't know well or will never see again?
    (b) Why or why not?

---

5. Why shouldn't someone steal from a store?
6. What is the value or importance of property rights?
7. (a) Should people do everything they can to obey the law?
   (b) Why or why not?
8. Was the old man being irresponsible by lending Bob the money?

Kohlberg's three levels and six stages of moral development

Level 1: Pre-conventional level No internalisation (up to about age 10).	Level 2: Conventional level Some internalisation (adolescence and early adulthood).	Level 3: Post-conventional level Full internalisation (most people never reach this stage).
Stage 1: **Heteronomous morality** Children obey because adults tell them to. Actions are determined by chance of external rewards or punishments.	**Stage 3:** **Mutual interpersonal expectations, relationships and interpersonal conformity** Children and adolescents value trust and loyalty. They adopt the moral standards of the significant adults around them, wishing to be seen as a good person by them.	**Stage 5:** **Social contract or utility and individual rights** People at this stage reason that certain values, rights and principles are sometimes more important than the laws of society. For example, Mary Kelly, a 51-year-old nurse and mother of four, decided to damage a US military aeroplane with an axe at Shannon Airport because she disagreed with US planes refuelling in Shannon en route to the war in Iraq, where US military aircraft were killing large numbers of innocent women and children.
Stage 2: **Individualism, purpose and exchange** The principle of equal exchange becomes important, e.g. it is all right to hit him because he hit me.	**Stage 4:** **Social systems morality** Adolescents at this stage begin to base their moral judgements on the need for social order, the law, justice and duty.	**Stage 6:** **Universal ethical principles** A person at this stage has developed a moral standard based on universal human rights. When faced with a decision between law and conscience, this person will follow conscience even if it brings personal risk. The case of Mary Kelly above could also fit in here.

(2) Moral behaviour

Moral behaviour is how an individual acts in morally challenging situations. As with the learning of social norms (see above), children learn their moral behaviour in two main ways: conditioning and by social modelling.

Conditioning and social modelling

At its simplest, when individuals are rewarded for moral behaviour, they are encouraged to repeat it, whereas when they are punished for behaviour that is morally wrong, they are encouraged not to. In reality, though, things are not as simple as this; if they were, then people would only ever spend one term in prison. Punishment is not a very effective tool. Skinner found that for punishment to be effective, it had to be severe enough to stop the undesirable behaviour and had to follow the undesirable behaviour straight afterwards. Severe immediate punishments are usually not possible or indeed desirable, so encouragement of moral behaviour is much more effective.

Bandura's social modelling theory (1977) also applies to moral development. Children who witness moral behaviour at home, in their communities and at school are much more likely to develop high moral standards themselves.

(3) Moral feeling

Moral feeling is how you react emotionally to moral decisions. Do you feel guilt when you do something morally suspect? Happy when you do something morally good? Does whether or not you are going to get found out have any bearing on your feelings?

Psychoanalytic theory of moral development

The famous psychoanalyst **Sigmund Freud (1856–1939)** spent many years exploring this aspect of personality. He believed that the personality was composed of three parts: the id, superego and ego.

- **Id:** This is the selfish, pleasure-seeking part of the personality. The id encourages the individual to satisfy its needs and does not consider consequences. During the first two years of life, a child's actions are almost exclusively governed by the id.
- **Superego:** This part of the personality is sometimes called the high priest. Moral teaching by parents, schools, the Church, the media and the community in which the child lives help form the superego. Because children are brought up in different environments, their superego can vary. For example, a child brought up in an environment where adults regularly get drunk may form the opinion that getting drunk regularly is morally fine.

- **Ego:** The ego is the part of the personality in touch with reality. The ego weighs up the pros and cons of carrying out a particular action and then makes a decision. It tries to balance the needs and wants of the id with the demands of the superego.

Look at the example opposite, which illustrates how the id, ego and superego interact.

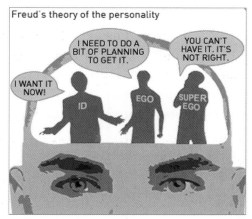

Id, ego and superego

While travelling home on the bus from school, Samantha notices a purse under the seat in front of her. She opens the purse and finds that there is €200 in cash in the purse along with some bank cards. What will Samantha do?

The id will want the €200 and will encourage Samantha to keep the purse. The superego will want Samantha to hand the purse in, as it is wrong to take it. The ego will weigh up the situation: Did anyone see me pick up the purse? If I hand the purse in to the driver, will he be honest or will he just keep the money? Do I need the money? What if the person who lost the purse really needs the money? What if I just keep some of the money or keep the money and give in the cards? Even if I hand it in, will it find its way back to the real owner? After considering all of these questions, Samantha will then make a decision. If she decides to take the money she may feel guilt, but only if her superego believes that what she has done is wrong.

Empathy

Empathy is another aspect of moral feeling. Empathy is not just sympathising with another person, it is feeling what someone else is feeling, putting yourself emotionally in their place. Damon (1988) proposes three stages in the development of empathy.

- **Global empathy** is characteristic of babies and toddlers (zero to two years). For example, if they see another child fall and hurt themselves, they may go out in sympathy, crying themselves, perhaps sucking their thumb and seeking comfort. It is as if they have been hurt themselves. This does not always happen, however; the toddler may just stand staring at the injured child, curious about what has happened to them.

- By early childhood, children can differentiate between their own hurt and that of others. By this stage they will also be able to empathise with another and respond appropriately, e.g. on the first day of school a little boy is very upset, so one of his classmates comes over, puts his arm around him and asks him if he wants to play with his toy soldiers.

- From approximately 10 to 12 years, children become capable of empathising with others even if they are not present with them, e.g. people living in poverty.

(4) Moral personality

Some people have strong morals and also have the strength to act on those moral convictions. A high standard of morality is part of their identity or how they view themselves. There is debate around how much of our moral personality is innate and how much is due to environment. Freud (see above) would contend that both are involved, with the id being present from birth and the ego and superego strongly influenced by environmental factors. There are individuals, however, who are reared in morally corrupt environments yet emerge from these environments morally strong. These cases lend weight to the nature argument, which states that moral personality is largely innate.

Influences on moral development

Parents

See also the section on parenting in Chapter 8.

While both Kohlberg and Piaget believed that peers have a much bigger influence on a child's moral development than adults, they did not deny that parents and other adults in the child's life have some influence. How much influence they have largely depends on three factors.

1. The quality of the adult–child relationship is very important. Children who are securely attached (see Chapter 8) and confident in their relationship with their parent or carer are much more likely to engage with them and respond to their moral guidance.
2. The form of discipline used by adults is also very important. Hoffman (1970) identified three different discipline techniques used by parents.
   - **Love withdrawal:** With this technique, the parent withholds attention or love from the child, perhaps refusing to talk to the child or saying to the child, 'I don't like you when you do that.'
   - **Power assertion:** The parent tries to gain control over the child and the child's resources. Examples include slapping or removing privileges.
   - **Induction:** The parent uses reasoning and explains the consequences of the child's actions to the child. An example would be saying, 'Don't hit him, he didn't mean to bump into you.' Of the three techniques, induction is seen to be the most effective. With love withdrawal and

power assertion, the child is likely to be highly anxious and aroused, thinking more about the punishment than the lesson behind it. With induction, the child is calm and more likely to take on board the reasoning behind what is being said.

3. Whether or not the parent is proactive. Being proactive means preventing misbehaviour before it takes place. With younger children, this may mean removing them from the situation or distracting them. With older children and adolescents, this may mean discussing the potential misbehaviour before it even happens, e.g. discussing smoking before children are offered a cigarette.

Preschools and schools

Within any school or preschool, both the explicit and the hidden curriculum exist. The explicit curriculum is usually written down and intended to be taught, whereas the hidden curriculum comprises the messages that the organisation sends out to the child that are not part of the explicit curriculum. In some ways, the hidden curriculum is even more important for moral development than the explicit curriculum. For example, if a teacher gives a lesson about the importance of keeping the environment litter free and the school is a litter black spot, then her message may not be heard.

In addition, it is important that preschools and schools advocate a **care perspective** for the promotion of moral development. Such a perspective concentrates on educating children about the importance of engaging in pro-social behaviours, such as considering the feelings of others, being sensitive to the needs of others and helping each other. This perspective ties in closely with the use of induction as a discipline technique (see above).

Special needs that affect social skills

Autistic spectrum disorders

Autistic spectrum disorder is the term used to describe a collection of developmental disorders primarily affecting a child's ability to communicate and form social relationships.

If a child is described as having **autism** this means that the child has a significant number of the developmental disorders listed on the autistic spectrum. Autism is considered the most severe of the autistic spectrum disorders. If a child is described as having **Asperger syndrome** they will have some of the developmental disorders listed on the autistic spectrum but not others. Autism and Asperger syndrome are the two conditions that will be dealt with briefly in this section, because of the difficulties both conditions cause in relation to social development.

Autism

Prevalence

While estimates for the prevalence of autism vary considerably, a recent Irish study estimated that the incidence of autism in Ireland is approximately 1 in 110 (Irish Autism Action 2012). It is more than four times more common in males and occurs equally among all racial groups.

Causes

Little is known about the causes of autism. It is believed that genetics plays a part because parents who have family members with autism are more likely to have a child with autism, and also some families have more than one child with autism.

Symptoms

Symptoms of autism centre around four areas:

- Severe communication difficulties (children with autism generally experience language delay and some remain non-verbal).
- Difficulty in social relationships.
- Repetitive activities and routines (children with autism may become upset if familiar routines are broken).
- Children with autism often have a narrow range of interests, which they may be quite obsessive about.

Children with autism benefit from early interventions. Applied Behaviour Analysis (ABA) is a teaching method, based on the work of B.F. Skinner, frequently used with children with autism to teach social and other skills.

Asperger syndrome

Asperger syndrome is an autism spectrum disorder that was first described by the Austrian paediatrician Hans Asperger in 1944. People with Asperger syndrome, like other conditions on the autistic spectrum, show significant difficulties in social interaction, along with restricted and repetitive patterns of behaviour and interests. Asperger syndrome differs from autism in that language and cognitive development is much less impaired. Also, although not required for diagnosis, physical clumsiness and atypical use of language are frequently reported. People with Asperger syndrome are often described by their peers as odd or eccentric.

Prevalence

In Ireland it is estimated that several thousand people have the syndrome, with about nine times as many males affected as females (Asperger Syndrome Association of Ireland 2009).

Causes

Asperger syndrome (AS) is believed to have a strong genetic component. Children with AS commonly have other immediate or extended family members with behavioural symptoms similar to AS, or a family history of depression or bipolar disorder. It is also associated, in some cases, with oxygen deprivation during the birth process.

Symptoms

The main symptoms of Asperger syndrome are:

1. **Impaired ability to interact socially:** Children with AS often experience difficulties with the basic skills required for social interaction. They may have difficulty making eye contact, have blank or unusual facial expressions and have difficulty showing empathy. Children with AS may also have unusual gestures, postures or ticks.

2. **Restricted and repetitive interests and behaviours:** Children with AS often display behaviour, interests and activities that are restricted and repetitive and are sometimes abnormally intense or focused. These interests often dominate social interaction so much that the person with AS will speak of little else. Repetitive hand movements such as flapping or twisting, and complex whole-body movements such as rocking or spinning are also usually present.

3. **Speech and language abnormalities:** Although individuals with Asperger syndrome acquire language skills without significant general delay, their speech has certain unusual characteristics that affect their ability to communicate effectively with others and thus their social development. One of the most important characteristics (mentioned earlier) is verbosity, also called prolixity. This means that the individual uses an excess of words. They will go off on long, wordy monologues, not realising that their listeners are not keeping up or are not interested in what they are saying.

People with AS also use quite literal speech and have difficulties understanding and using things like metaphor, such as 'The Government toppled like a house of cards', or figurative speech, such as 'I nearly died laughing'. Children with AS appear to have particular weaknesses in areas of non-literal language that include humour, irony and good-natured teasing.

People with AS may also have what is called **auditory processing deficits.** This means that sometimes the child will have difficulty 'hearing' what is being said to them despite normal physical hearing. A child may for example hear little of what their teacher is saying to the general class, only hearing what she is saying when she is speaking directly to him or her. Children with AS may use unusually formal speech and may also use unusual intonation, e.g. their voice may be flatter than normal or they may use an inappropriate pitch and loudness while talking.

Social stories

Social stories are very important for children who have difficultly developing social skills, including children on the autistic spectrum. Many social skills are learned by children by simply copying what they see. Some children, however, require more explicit instructions and find the use of social stories very beneficial. Social stories present children with day-to-day occurrences that may be challenging for them. Children then act out the social story, which gives them practice with social skills.

Example of a social story: *Asking someone to play*

(stories may be illustrated)

My name is _____ and I like to play with other kids.

At break time there are lots of kids from my class that I can play with.

When I want to play with someone I need to do these things.

First I need to look at their face.

Next I need to say their name to get their attention.

I then wait until that person looks back at me.

Then I say 'Can I play with you?'

If the person says 'yes' then I get to play with this person.

If they say 'no' then it is OK, I can find another person to ask.

It makes me feel happy that I know how to ask someone to play.

Pro-social and antisocial behaviour in children

Pro-social behaviour

Pro-social behaviour means being concerned for the rights and welfare of others, being able to empathise and act in ways that benefit others. Learning to share with others is one of the earliest forms of pro-social behaviour that children demonstrate.

William Damon (1988) suggests that up until about the age of three, children share because it is something they have been taught they must do and not generally for empathic reasons. From approximately four years, however, children begin to share because they feel empathy for the other child, but generally will only share if they have more than enough for themselves and if what they are sharing is not too coveted. The important thing about sharing in terms of social development is that the child understands that sharing is an important part of forming and maintaining social relationships and that it is morally right to share.

Developing a sense of fairness is another concept that is an important part of developing pro-social behaviour. Fairness is usually defined in terms of equality (that everyone is treated equally), merit (extra rewards come to those who work hard for them) and benevolence (special consideration should be given to those who need something most). Up until children are about eight years of age, they think of fairness in terms of equality only. From about eight years on, they can begin to think of it in terms of merit and benevolence as well. Studies that seek to understand how children understand the concept of fairness suggest that children learn considerably more from their peers in this regard than from the adults in their lives. Pro-social behaviour generally develops sooner in girls than boys.

Antisocial behaviour

Most children act out from time to time and on occasion act in a destructive and troublesome way. If children do so on a regular basis, however, and their behaviour is interfering with their peer relationships, relationships with adults around them and usually their educational progress, they may be showing signs of one of a number of emotional and/or behavioural disorders.

Oppositional defiant disorder (ODD)

With ODD, the child shows a recurrent and unusual pattern of negative, defiant, disobedient and hostile behaviour towards adult authority figures in particular. For ODD to be diagnosed, the behaviour must have continued for at least six months with four or more of the following symptoms present:

- Often loses temper.
- Often argues with adults.
- Often actively defies/refuses to comply with adults' requests or rules.
- Often deliberately annoys people.
- Often puts the blame for own mistakes or behaviour on others.
- Often is easily upset or annoyed by others.
- Often is angry and resentful.
- Often is spiteful and vindictive.

These behaviours cause a significant impairment to social and academic functioning. Children with ODD are often shunned by peers because of their behaviour and frequently fall behind academically due to the fact that much of their energy is spent opposing playgroup leaders and teachers rather than carrying out the tasks set for them. Children with ODD also tend to spend periods of time excluded from their groups. Children with ODD usually possess a 'counter-will', meaning the more one tries to have the child behave appropriately, the more opposition is experienced. It is very rare for a child to have ODD alone. ODD may appear with ADHD (see Chapter 5), depression, conduct disorder (see below), bipolar disorder, Tourette syndrome or other special educational needs.

Conduct disorder

Conduct disorder (CD) is often incorrectly diagnosed at first as ODD. With conduct disorder, however, behaviours are much more destructive and extreme. A child with conduct disorder seems to be unable to consider the feelings of others and will frequently hurt or injure others and appear to think it is funny. CD is much more common in boys than girls and can escalate to very serious levels as the child gets older. Children with CD have been known to kill and maim pets, bully and intimidate their peers, steal, damage property and set fires. Like ODD, CD rarely occurs alone. While the exact cause of CD is not known, it is believed that three factors are involved: genetic inheritance of an aggressive temperament, poor parenting skills and growing up in an environment where violence is normalised.

Effective management of children's behaviour

- Adults should intervene and help peers and siblings sort out differences in a calm and fair manner.
- If one child hurts another, always encourage the offending child to think about how the other one feels.
- Encourage children to manage their anger, e.g. count to 10.
- Reinforce social norms with praise and encouragement, e.g. saying, 'Yes, good girl, we always wash our hands after going to the toilet.'
- Always seek to encourage good behaviour rather than punish bad behaviour.
- Set clear yet fair rules and boundaries for children to follow.
- Practise what you preach, e.g. if a parent asks a child not to hit others, then they should not slap the child.
- Use induction as a discipline technique – reason with the child and discuss the consequences of their actions with the child.
- Advocate a care perspective. Teach the importance of considering others' feelings, being sensitive to the needs of others and helping others.

- When children misbehave, use positive discipline techniques. Wrongdoing should be discussed with the child, and a plan put in place to prevent it happening again. In this way behaviour management is always forward-looking.

- The Maltese physician and author Edward de Bono (1933–) makes a very interesting point in relation to dealing with differences of opinion. When a child, particularly an older child, has a disagreement with an adult, e.g. a teacher, very often the child is not really listening to the adult's point of view and vice versa. De Bono suggests that a discussion should happen whereby the adult asks the child, 'What do you think I am thinking, and I will tell you what I think you are thinking?' In this way the two parties can actively try to see things from the other's point of view in a more democratic way.

- One very interesting and important aspect of William Glasser's (1925–) **Choice theory** is the issue of power. He believed that one reason some children misbehaved in school environments was that the environment made them feel powerless. Giving children choices at school or pre-school helps alleviate power inequalities. For example, children are given a choice of three Christmas cards to make. They can choose whichever one they like best.

How Aistear promotes social development

Promotion of social development is at the very heart of the Aistear curriculum and its approach to working with young children. One of its main pedagogical principles is that **children learn through positive interactions with others**. Aistear's guidelines for good practice state that:

> Aistear recognises that relationships are at the very centre of early learning and development. The good practice guidelines identify a range of interaction strategies and methods the adult can use to enhance children's learning and development. Effective interactions between adults and children need to be **respectful, playful, enjoyable, enabling,** and **rewarding**.
>
> (NCCA 2009: 27)

All of Aistear's four themes have elements of social development within them. The table below shows what Aistear sets out to do in relation to the promotion of social development in the early years. Early years practitioners take these aims and learning goals and provide unstructured and structured play opportunities designed to fulfil these aims and goals.

Theme: Well-being	
Aims	**Learning goals**
Aim 1: Children will be strong psychologically and socially.	In partnership with the adult, children will: 1. make strong attachments and develop warm and supportive relationships with family, peers and adults in out-of-home settings and in their community 2. be aware of and name their own feelings, and understand that others may have different feelings 3. handle transitions and changes well 4. be confident and self-reliant 5. respect themselves, others and the environment 6. make decisions and choices about their own learning and development.
Theme: Identity and belonging	
Aims	**Learning goals**
Aim 1: Children will have strong self-identities and will feel respected and affirmed as unique individuals with their own life stories.	In partnership with the adult, children will: 1. build respectful relationships with others 2. appreciate the features that make a person special and unique (name, size, hair, hand and footprint, gender, birthday) 3. understand that as individuals they are separate from others with their own needs, interests and abilities 4. have a sense of 'who they are' and be able to describe their backgrounds, strengths and abilities 5. feel valued and see themselves and their interests reflected in the environment 6. express their own ideas, preferences and needs, and have these responded to with respect and consistency.
Aim 2: Children will have a sense of group identity where links with their family and community are acknowledged and extended.	In partnership with the adult, children will: 1. feel that they have a place and a right to belong to the group 2. know that members of their family and community are positively acknowledged and welcomed 3. be able to share personal experiences about their own families and cultures, and come to know that there is a diversity of family structures, cultures and backgrounds 4. understand and take part in routines, customs, festivals, and celebrations 5. see themselves as part of a wider community and know about their local area, including some of its places, features and people 6. understand the different roles of people in the community.

Aim 3: Children will be able to express their rights and show an understanding and regard for the identity, rights and views of others.	In partnership with the adult, children will:
	1. express their views and help make decisions in matters that affect them
	2. understand the rules and the boundaries of acceptable behaviour
	3. interact, work co-operatively, and help others
	4. be aware of and respect others' needs, rights, feelings, culture, language, background and religious beliefs
	5. have a sense of social justice and recognise and deal with unfair behaviour
	6. demonstrate the skills of co-operation, responsibility, negotiation, and conflict resolution.
Aim 4: Children will see themselves as capable learners.	In partnership with the adult, children will:
	2. show an awareness of their own unique strengths, abilities and learning styles, and be willing to share their skills and knowledge with others.
Theme: Communicating	
Aims	**Learning goals**
Aim 1: Children will use non-verbal communication skills.	In partnership with the adult, children will:
	1. use a range of body movements, facial expressions, and early vocalisations to show feelings and share information
	2. understand and use non-verbal communication rules, such as turn-taking and making eye contact
	3. interpret and respond to non-verbal communication by others
	4. understand and respect that some people will rely on non-verbal communication as their main way of interacting with others
	5. combine non-verbal and verbal communication to get their point across
	6. express themselves creatively and imaginatively using non-verbal communication.
Aim 2: Children will use language.	In partnership with the adult, children will
	1. interact with other children and adults by listening, discussing and taking turns in conversation.

(NCCA 2009: 17, 26, 35)

Sample observation

Observation 4: Social development

Date of observation: 29 November 2013

Time observation started and finished: 12.30–13.00

Number of children present: 65 (approximately)

Number of adults present: 1 teacher, 1 SNA, 1 student (observer)

Permission obtained from: Teacher

Description of setting: This observation took place at lunchtime in the yard of a rural primary school. The yard is quite large and with a tarmac surface. Junior and senior infants together with first class play in this part of the yard, with bigger classes around the back of the school. There are some games, e.g. hopscotch and snakes and ladders, stencilled onto the tarmac. The children generally play with these, or play chasing or play with a light football provided.

Immediate context: This observation took place just after the children ate their lunch and were sent out to play in the yard. There is a teacher and an SNA on duty, supervising the children at play. At the beginning of the observation, TC is standing at the wall of a bike shed watching the boys from his class and junior infants play football.

Brief description of the child observed: TC is a male aged five years and 10 months old. He is currently in senior infants and is one of he oldest in his class. He is very shy and quiet and much smaller than many of the boys in his class. TC has learning difficulties and his speech is sometimes difficult to understand. TC does not often play with other children, and frequently comes to staff telling on other children, e.g. child X said a bad word.

Aim of observation: The aim of this observation is to observe TC for five-minute intervals over a period of 30 minutes in order to assess his social development.

Rationale: TC seems to be having difficulties joining in with other children, especially when an adult is not structuring the activities, e.g. at lunchtime. TC frequently (every few minutes) reports to staff that other children have done something wrong, e.g. used bad language. TC also has a number of antisocial habits, e.g. picking his nose. It is important to observe TC interacting with other children in order to get a clear picture of what is actually going on so that a plan can be put in place to encourage TC to interact more effectively with his peers.

Method: Time sample

Media used: Pen, prepared time sample grid, clipboard

	Observation		
Time	**Actions**	**Social group**	**Language**
12.30	Standing at the side of a bike shed looking towards senior infants and first class playing ball.	On own.	Not speaking.
12.35	Walking towards teacher and SNA, then walking back to child X.	Teacher and SNA, two first class girls also present.	'Teacher, child X (says name of child) has his roll, Teacher, child X has his roll.' Teacher says, 'Tell child X he shouldn't be eating his roll outside, he'll choke on it.'
12.40	Standing watching girls play with stencils on the ground. TC is picking his nose constantly and putting it into his mouth.	On own, near group of five senior infant girls playing a form of hopscotch on the ground.	Girls are talking away among themselves but do not speak to TC, who is standing quite close to them. TC does not attempt to speak to them.
12.45	TC has joined a group of senior infant boys who are running in a row up and down the playground.	TC is running along with a group of six other senior infant boys.	TC is not speaking. Most of the other children are shouting to each other.
12.50	TC is walking up to the teacher and SNA again to tell on child X (the same child as before). TC walks back and tells child X to come over to the teacher.	Teacher.	TC says, 'Teacher, child X said a bad word.' Teacher says, 'Tell child X I want to talk to him.' Teacher says to child X, 'No bad language, child X, now off you go.'
12.55	TC is walking around the perimeter of the playground, scraping the tops of his shoes on the ground.	TC is on his own.	Not speaking.
1.00	Children have lined up to go back inside. TC is toward the back of the line and is lightly kicking at the back of the legs of the child in front of him.	TC is in line with a large number of peers. There is a boy to the front and back of him.	Child Y (in front of TC) turns round and says, 'Stop that, TC, stop.' TC smiles and kicks child Y again once. When child Y turns round again, TC says, 'Sorry.' Child Z, who is standing behind TC, says, 'TC, that's stupid.'

Evaluation

(See Chapter 4, p. 93 for a note on the structure of evaluations.)

The aim of this observation was to observe TC over the lunchtime period in order to assess his social development. TC seems to be having some difficulty interacting effectively with his peers, so it was therefore important to observe how he is interacting in a systematic way over a period of time so as to put a plan in place for him.

Social development essentially involves the development of three sets of skills: an ability to interact effectively with others, an understanding of the norms of society and moral development (Flood 2013). Generally, TC seems to be having difficultly in all three of these areas.

At the beginning of this observation, TC is standing on his own near the bike shed watching his peers playing ball. He makes no attempt to join in. TC seems to have difficulty joining peer groups in play, especially if he has to interact or speak. TC was able to join his peers when they were just running up and down the yard. From about four years, children 'begin to try to work out how to integrate themselves smoothly into peer activities and to begin friendships with selected peers' (Flood 2013). TC is almost six years old and does not seem to be able to do this very successfully yet.

TC does understand the rules of the school and frequently tells on others if they break them. He is very much at Piaget's heteronomous stage of morality, where everything is black and white and rules are handed down from on high, in this case from the teacher. During this observation, he went to the teacher and told on another child twice. He reported the first time that a child was eating a roll in the playground and the second time that they had said a bad word. This is very usual behaviour for TC and makes him unpopular with his peers. Wentzel and Asher (1995), after interviewing large groups of schoolchildren, found that children can be categorised into five different peer group statuses – popular, average, neglected, rejected and controversial children. TC would probably fall into the 'rejected' category. This may be because he constantly tells on others, does not understand some social norms (see below) and also cries frequently. This would fit with Wentzel and Asher's (1995) description of rejected children. They found in general that rejected children find it difficult to consider things from someone else's perspective (TC does not consider what it is like to be told on), cannot process social information (TC acts inappropriately, kicking the child in front of him in the line and then smiling) and are not able to regulate their emotions. While TC did not cry or get angry during this observation, he often does.

Social norms 'are descriptions or "rules" about people's behaviour, beliefs, attitudes and values within a society or social group' (Flood 2013). Using a tissue to clean your nose is a social norm in our society. TC does not seem to understand this and picks his nose quite openly, much to the annoyance of his peers.

In general, TC's social development seems to be somewhat behind the norms for his age group. He seems to have difficulty interacting appropriately with his peers or joining in with games. He seems to try to get peer attention the wrong way, e.g. kicking them. He does not seem to understand some societal norms, e.g. cleaning your nose in a tissue. TC does understand rules, but sees them in a very black and white manner. Any time one of his peers breaks a rule, TC feels that he should report it to the teacher. This is making him unpopular with his peers.

Personal learning gained

- I learned a good deal more about children's social development. I learned that social development is composed of three elements: interacting with others, understanding the norms of society and moral development. Before this, I would have thought social development meant interacting with peers only.
- I learned about the importance of objectively observing children. Through observation, important issues can be highlighted more precisely and a plan put in place to help the child develop the skills they need.
- I learned about Piaget's theory of moral development. He proposed that morality develops in two stages and that children under seven years are generally at stage one – heteronomous morality.

Recommendations

- TC is almost six years of age, but is not yet very good at integrating himself into peer activities. Perhaps TC could be taught this skill directly, e.g. using social stories.
- Practitioners should reinforce social norms with TC, e.g. telling him to use a tissue for his nose.

References

Flood, E. (2013), *Child Development for Students in Ireland* (2nd edn.). Dublin, Gill & Macmillan.

Santrock, J. (2009), *Child Development* (12th edn.). New York: McGraw-Hill.

Wentzel, K. and Asher, S. (1995), 'The Academic Lives of Neglected, Rejected, Popular and Controversial Children', *Child Development*, 66, 754–63.

Signatures

Sandra Boyle   Date: <u>29/11/2013</u>
Student

Jessica Little   Date: <u>21/11/2013</u>
Supervisor

Jacinta Gillespie   Date: <u>5/12/2013</u>
Tutor

Revision questions

1. What is social development?
2. What is meant by parallel play?
3. Describe how children's ability to interact effectively with others develops from birth to six years.

(Questions 4–9: FETAC Level 6 only)

4. Describe how children's ability to interact effectively with others develops from birth to 12 years.
5. Describe the types of bullying children may be subjected to.
6. What are the factors that make a child more likely to engage in bullying behaviour?
7. What signs could indicate that a child is being bullied?
8. What can schools do to help prevent bullying?
9. What advice can parents and schools give children who are being bullied?

10. According to Dunn (2007), what are the three main characteristics of sibling relationships?
11. Should parents intervene in sibling fights?
12. What three skills are necessary for successful peer relations?
13. How do Wentzel and Asher (1995) classify children's peer status?
14. What are social norms?
15. Describe the behaviourist view of how children learn social norms.
16. What is meant by social modelling?
17. Name the four different aspects of moral development.
18. Describe Piaget's theory of moral development.

19. Describe Kohlberg's theory of moral development.
20. Describe Freud's psychoanalytic theory of moral development.
21. What is empathy?
22. Describe Damon's three stages in the development of empathy.
23. Describe how parents can influence their child's moral development.
24. In schools and pre-schools, what is the difference between the explicit and hidden curriculum?
25. How can schools and pre-schools promote moral development?
26. Define both pro-social and antisocial behaviour.
27. Describe one special need that affects social development.
28. What is oppositional defiant disorder?
29. What is conduct disorder?
30. How can pre-schools and schools deal effectively with children's challenging behaviour?

Emotional Development

What is emotional development?

An **emotion** can be described as a mental and physiological state associated with a wide variety of feelings, thoughts and behaviour. Because the same situation can affect people differently, emotions are subjective experiences, often associated with mood, temperament, personality and cultural differences. Examples of emotions include anger, joy, jealousy, fear, love, sadness, shyness, frustration, distress, pride, worry, contentment and disgust. **Emotional development** is the development of the ability to recognise and deal with emotions in a positive, healthy and socially acceptable way. For example, a two-year-old toddler must learn that they cannot fly into a temper tantrum each time their request for something desirable is denied.

Emotions can be classified into **primary emotions**, e.g. joy, fear, disgust, anger, sadness and surprise, and **self-conscious emotions** (sometimes called **other-conscious emotions**), e.g. jealousy, shame, pride, guilt, empathy and embarrassment. While primary emotions appear in the first six months, self-conscious emotions generally do not appear until after six months because in order to experience these emotions the child has to have a sense of 'self' in relation to others. Jealousy and pride are normally the first to appear, with others appearing more towards the end of the second year.

In terms of emotional expression, crying is the primary way babies less than five or six weeks old express emotion. After six weeks, when the social smile first appears, babies begin to expand their repertoire and begin to be able to express joy, surprise and sadness. Fear as an emotion typically appears around six months with the emergence of **stranger anxiety**. Stranger anxiety usually gets more intense as the child gets older, peaking between 15 and 18 months. Closely related to stranger anxiety is **separation distress** or **separation protest**. This is when the infant gets very upset when their main carer leaves. While patterns of separation distress vary between cultures (because of variations in childminding arrangements), it usually appears from six months, getting stronger and peaking at approximately 15 months.

Emotional regulation is an important part of emotional development. From early infancy, babies do exhibit some emotion regulatory actions, e.g. sucking their thumb, but most emotional regulation is external in nature, e.g. an adult rocks and sings to a crying baby. Adults should try to soothe infants before they get into a very agitated state, as this helps the infant regulate their emotions and reduces the levels of stress hormones released. Babies should not be left to cry, as responding quickly to the infant in the first year of life is important for secure emotional attachments (see below). Studies of babies whose mothers responded promptly to them crying at three months cried less at a year than babies of mothers who did not respond promptly (Bell and Ainsworth 1972).

As children get older, they begin to experience a wider range of emotions during their day. They begin to be able to regulate their emotions more effectively, no longer relying as heavily on external regulators such as parents and carers to do so. They become better able to interpret other people's emotional states and how to deal effectively with them, e.g. how to show sympathy for another. As language emerges, children begin to be able to describe emotions and in this way can say how they feel about something rather than just act it out. From about four to five years, children begin to realise that emotional regulation is necessary to meet social standards. As discussed in Chapter 7, children who fail to regulate their emotions may experience rejection by their peers and have difficulty forming friendships.

Influence of temperament on emotional development

Over the years, a number of studies have been carried out categorising infants' temperaments and investigating the extent to which temperament is either inherited or emerges as a result of environmental influences. These studies are important in terms of understanding emotional development because a baby's temperament, whether it is easy or difficult, may have a bearing on how that baby is treated and as a result influence their emotional development.

In a longitudinal study of infant temperament, psychiatrists Stella Thomas and Alexander Chess (1977) found that three basic temperament types emerge:

- **Easy babies** (40 per cent): These babies are generally very positive, cry very little and quickly get into sleep and feeding routines. They adapt well to change.
- **Difficult babies** (10 per cent): These babies cry frequently, are slow to get into sleep and feeding routines and do not like change.
- **Slow to warm up babies** (15 per cent): These babies are not very active, and are often negative in terms of mood.

Thomas and Chess found that they were unable to clearly classify 35 per cent of the babies they studied.

Goodness of fit is an important concept related to studies of children's temperament. If a baby has a difficult temperament, their difficult temperament will only negatively affect their emotional development if the people caring for them react negatively to their temperament. If, on the other hand, there is a goodness of fit, i.e. their carers are patient and positive towards them despite their difficult temperament, then being a 'difficult baby' should not adversely affect emotional development.

Attachment theory

Attachment is a close emotional bond between a child and his or her carer. Strong or secure attachments are considered vital to healthy emotional development and are generally fostered in the first two years of life. John Bowlby (1969) argues that infants are born predisposed to form attachments. They cry, coo, smile and later crawl and walk after their carer. All of these behaviours are designed to keep their carer nearby and them safe from harm. Schaffer (1996) believes that attachment behaviours emerge gradually over four phases during the course of the first two years of life:

- **Zero to two months:** The baby cries and from five or six weeks will smile (but at anyone who smiles and chats to them).
- **Two to seven months:** The baby focuses its attachment behaviours on one or two people, known as their **primary attachment figure(s)**. The baby becomes able to distinguish familiar from unfamiliar people. They show a preference for familiars, smiling more and calming down more easily for familiars if upset.
- **Seven to 24 months:** Specific attachments develop. The baby will actively seek contact with their primary attachment figures, crawling or walking after them. Separation anxiety emerges in that the baby will become upset if they are left to be cared for by someone other than their primary attachment figures.
- **From 24 months:** Children begin to become aware of others' feelings, goals and plans and start to take these into account, e.g. 'Mammy has to go to work now, I'll be back to pick you up later.'

Differences in attachment behaviours

Mary Ainsworth (1979) studied differences in the quality of babies' attachments to their mothers. This was done by evaluating infant behaviour in what she called the **strange situation**. In the strange situation, the infant and mother play together in a room; the infant is free to explore and play with toys in the room. A stranger then enters the room and tries to interact with the infant. Some time later, the mother leaves the room, returning after a period of time. The infant's reactions to all of this are observed and recorded. Ainsworth categorised infants in one of four ways:

- **Securely attached:** These infants used the mother as a secure base from which to freely explore the room and examine the toys available. They were not unduly worried by the stranger entering the room. When the mother left the room they protested mildly, seeking to follow. When she returned they sought to re-establish contact, smiling and sometimes climbing up on her lap.
- **Insecure avoidant:** These infants show insecurity by avoiding the mother. They interact little with her, are not distressed when she leaves the room and do not seek comfort from her on her return. If the mother tries to make contact, the baby may lean or look away.
- **Insecure resistant:** These infants cling to the mother but at the same time fight the closeness by kicking or pushing her away. These infants in the strange situation clung to their mother and explored the playroom very little. They cried loudly and persistently when the mother left the room and pushed her away when she tried to comfort them on her return.
- **Insecure disorganised:** The infants are disorganised and disorientated. In the strange situation, they appeared fearful and confused. To be classified as insecure disorganised, babies had to show strong avoidance of their mother or extreme fearfulness.

Effects of early attachments on later emotional development

Harry Harlow's studies of maternal deprivation

In what would nowadays be considered an ethically unacceptable series of experiments, Harry Harlow (1958) studied the effects of maternal deprivation on rhesus monkeys by separating large numbers of baby monkeys from their natural mothers at birth and isolating them, giving them no contact with other monkeys. Because rhesus monkeys share some 98 per cent of their genetic material with humans, he believed that his experiments would shed light on human attachment behaviours and the effects of maternal deprivation. Some monkeys were reared by milk-producing wire surrogate mothers while others had two mothers – a milk-producing wire one and a cloth one that produced no milk. Harlow found that babies clung to the cloth mother for up to 15 hours per day and only went to the wire mother to feed.

When these monkeys were returned to the group, they were anxious, fearful and had difficulty forming relationships. They did not wish to breed and when they were forced to do so they frequently mistreated their young, sometimes killing them.

Harlow later developed a cloth mother that he called the iron maiden. She shot spikes and cold water at her babies, often injuring them. The babies continued to return to her even though she abused them. These monkeys were very disturbed, rocking back and forth; one even chewed off its own hand. None of these monkeys made even adequate parents, with most killing their offspring.

While most people object strongly to Harlow's methods, his findings are considered significant to human child development, particularly in relation to the effects of inadequate or abusive mothering on children's social relationships and future parenting skills.

Harry Harlow experiment of baby monkey clinging to cloth mother

Evaluation of attachment theories

While attachment theory is widely accepted as having great significance for healthy social and emotional development, aspects of attachment theory have also been criticised.

- **The mother as sole attachment figure:** Much of the work on infant attachment focuses exclusively on babies and their mothers. In modern society, babies are often cared for by others, e.g. there are currently 7,000 stay-at-home dads in Ireland according to 2008 figures from the Central Statistics Office.

- **The strange situation:** The strange situation used by Ainsworth to categorise infants is considered by some as being 'too strange'. These experiments were carried out in laboratory settings with which the child was unfamiliar, which could cause infants to behave in ways unnatural to them.

- **Culturally specific:** Much of the work carried out on attachment theory has been conducted in America and England, not taking into account differences in childrearing practices. For example, in many agricultural-based societies, babies are cared for shortly after birth by older siblings and grandparents. In north German society, babies are encouraged to be independent from a young age, possibly explaining why a larger than usual proportion of German children are classified as insecure avoidant. In Japanese society, mothers are not encouraged to allow anybody else to care for their baby, which possibly explains why a larger than usual proportion of Japanese babies are classified as insecure resistant.

- **Finality of attachment:** Some psychologists, e.g. Kagan (1987), believe that attachment theorists place too much emphasis on early attachments. He argues that children are adaptive and just because they do not have strong emotional attachments in infancy does not mean that they will not develop them later in life.

Despite these criticisms, secure attachments are seen as important for overall child development. It is important that children are cared for by a small number of consistent, caring adults, particularly during the first two years of life.

Psychoanalytic theories of personality development
Sigmund Freud (1856–1939)

Sigmund Freud is widely regarded as the father of psychoanalysis (see also Chapter 7, page 156).

In relation to emotional development, Freud's theories regarding the unconscious mind are very interesting. He proposed that the mind is divided into three areas – the unconscious mind, the preconscious and the conscious mind. The conscious mind contains thoughts and sensations that we are fully aware of; the preconscious mind contains thoughts and sensations that we can bring to consciousness with effort, for example you meet someone in town and cannot bring their name to mind, yet you know you know it. Later that day you remember their name. For the period you could not bring the name to mind this fact was in the preconscious.

He believed the unconscious mind to be the most influential in the formation of personality and in emotional development. He likened the unconscious mind to an enormous storehouse holding all the thoughts, feelings, experiences and emotions from an individual's past. Many of these thoughts and feelings could not or would not ever be brought to consciousness.

His theory in this regard was that much of our behaviour and personality is determined by the contents of our unconscious mind and that humans suppress feelings or thoughts that cause them anxiety using a variety of defence mechanisms. These defence mechanisms include denial, displacement, repression, regression, sublimation and projection. The preconscious mind can sometimes be involved in these defence mechanisms.

Freud felt that personality change is difficult because so much of our personality is driven by the unconscious.

Some of Freud's defence mechanisms:

Denial: Denying or avoiding an unpleasant thought or feeling, e.g. a child who has difficulty reading may go to the toilet during reading time.

Displacement: Redirecting negative feelings onto a safe target, e.g. a child is being bullied at school by another child; they come home and bully a younger sibling.

Repression:	The mind pushes unpleasant thoughts or experiences down into the unconscious mind, e.g. some adults who have been abused as children cannot remember the abuse because they have repressed it.
Regression:	Going back to a time when the problem did not exist, e.g. a child who is toilet-trained may go back to wetting or soiling themselves upon the arrival of a new sibling.
Rationalisation:	Trying to justify what is going on through rational argument or making excuses, e.g. someone who is drinking too much may justify what they are doing by saying they need to relax because of their very heavy workload.
Reaction formation:	A person behaves in the opposite way to how they feel, e.g. a child who is being bullied may begin to speak and act very aggressively.
Projection:	Unacceptable thoughts or feelings are projected onto others, e.g. a woman has an affair and beings to gossip about other women, calling them 'tarts' etc.
Sublimation:	This is one of the few healthy defence mechanisms. It occurs when an individual displaces their negative thoughts and feelings in a positive or healthy way, e.g. going for a run, drawing or painting.

Anna Freud (FETAC Level 6 only)

Anna Freud (1895–1982) was the sixth and last child of Sigmund and Martha Freud. Like her father Anna was very interested in the area of psychoanalysis. With the outbreak of World War I, Anna travelled with her father and the rest of her family to London. Here she founded the Hampstead War Nursery (renamed the Anna Freud Centre after her death). She also worked after the war in the Bulldog's Bank Home, an orphanage for child concentration camp survivors. Through this work Anna observed first-hand children who had experienced very distressing childhoods.

Anna built on her father's work, particularly with regard to the importance of the ego in warding off displeasure and anxiety, in identifying additional defence mechanisms. She published a paper in 1936 entitled 'The ego and the mechanisms of defence'. Unlike her father, who believed that most defence mechanisms were unconscious (the individual is not aware they are using them), she believed that some of them are conscious and can be controlled by the individual, e.g. thought suppression – deciding not to think about something because it is unpleasant.

Anna, much more so than her father, was interested in children from latency period onwards. While her father believed that our personalities are pretty much a reflection of our unconscious minds, Anna placed much greater importance on the value of the intellect. She believed that we can think about how we feel and make conscious efforts to change.

She believed that daydreaming was a necessary part of childhood and that sometimes it is used as a substitute for unacceptable impulses. As part of her work Anna was very interested in the effects of parental deprivation. Many of the children she worked with had witnessed their parents being killed or tortured in concentration camps. She found that many of these children survived remarkably well emotionally and that the comfort and support these children gave to each other was the main reason for this. She believed that play was a very important aspect of childhood, particularly when used to alleviate anxiety or tension. Anna also believed that children should talk and think through what is causing them anxiety. She was therefore in favour of adults taking time to observe and talk to children if they seem anxious or worried.

Melanie Klein 1880–1960

Melanie Klein came to London in 1926, before Sigmund and Anna Freud. While she supported much of their work in relation to psychoanalytic theory she disagreed in other ways, for example she disagreed with Freud regarding the importance of sexual desire and with Anna Freud's methods of using psychoanalysis with children. Klein is probably best known for her use of **play therapy** with children to help them overcome emotional and behavioural problems. Her methods are still being used today. Play therapy provides a way for children to express their experiences and feelings through a natural, self-guided, self-healing process. Klein used all sorts of play equipment including small world toys, clay, sand, puppets, art and craft materials, toys soldiers and guns.

D.W. Winnicott (1896–1971)

Donald Woods Winnicott was a very influential and important English paediatrician and psychoanalyst. He was born into a well known and prosperous family; his father Sir John Frederick Winnicott was knighted in 1924. Winnicott however did not have an easy childhood; his mother, Elizabeth Martha Woods Winnicott, suffered severely with depression and he felt very protective and responsible for her. He remembered as a child 'trying to make my living by keeping my mother alive' (Winnicott in Minsky 1996: 134).

Winnicott trained as a doctor and after qualifying began working at Paddington Green Children's Hospital as a paediatrician and child psychoanalyst, a position he held for the next forty years. Winnicott was a contemporary of both Anna Freud and Melanie Klein, in fact he studied psychoanalysis under Klein for a number of years. Later, though, he began developing his own independent ideas, for which he is now well known.

Like Anna Freud and Melanie Klein, Winnicott worked with young people displaced by war and also children coming from dysfunctional families. It is through this work that he came up with the concept of the 'good-enough mother' (Winnicott referred mainly to the child's mother, probably reflecting the fact that most women did not work outside the home when he was forming his theories). He realised very early on that there is no such thing as a perfect mother but that a 'good-enough mother' will have characteristics that are important to healthy psychological development. Likewise by talking to and studying the lives of children experiencing psychological problems he was able to identify aspects of their lives that he believed lay behind their difficulties.

The concept of holding

Winnicott believed that babies and children need to be frequently and attentively held by their mothers. Mothers are a baby's security blanket, providing frequent and affectionate handling. Later this broadens to other people in the child's world, but initially he believed the mother to be the important figure. The concept of holding means not only physically holding the child but also anything the mother, and later family and wider society, do to make the child feel secure and 'held'. Winnicott observed that this 'concept of holding' was absent from the lives of many children he worked with causing what he termed an 'anti-social tendency'. He believed that if children do not feel secure at home they will seek security elsewhere, e.g. within gangs. He says in his work *The Child, the Family and the Outside World* that:

> . . a child whose home fails to give a feeling of security looks outside his home for the four walls . . . looking to society instead of his own family or school to provide the stability he needs.

(Winnicott 1973)

False and real self

Winnicott believed that none of us is born with a clear sense of self and that it develops as we grow. In this way Winnicott is very much an advocate of the nurture side of the nature vs. nurture debate. He did not believe that we are born with a certain type of personality, rather that our personality grows over time, and is very much influenced by our environment.

Winnicott was very interested in the concept or idea of the 'premature development of the ego function'. Winnicott believed that when children have to grow up too fast (their ego is forced to develop too quickly) their psychological development suffers and a 'false self' is created. This could happen, for example, if the eldest child of dysfunctional parents has to care for younger siblings on a daily basis. As his own mother had depression during his childhood Winnicott was interested in the effects that this and other family problems have on children. He believed that problems such as this caused a phenomenon he called 'compliance'. The child tries to solve the problem by being 'good'. In adulthood his or her actions will always be motivated out of a desire to please others. This leaves the person open to abuse and being used by others.

On the other hand children who experience 'good-enough' parenting grow up trusting their world and are therefore free to be their 'true self' most of the time. Winnicott believed that in reality we are all a mix of both our 'true' and 'false' selves, but that as long as the 'false' self does not take over we will be psychologically healthy. He realised that as part of life sometimes we have to 'people please'.

Transitional object

Winnicott is well known for his belief in what he called 'transitional objects' or comfort objects, such as a teddy bear or blanket. He believed that these objects were very useful and important in helping a child cope with transitions, for instance, separation from their mother when she returns to work after maternity leave.

Importance of play

Unlike many other psychoanalysts Winnicott saw play as being vital and central to healthy development. He believed that being a 'good-enough mother' involved being a playful mother and that playing games, such as peek-a-boo, is essential. Winnicott believed that play is vital throughout life, even in adulthood, as it is an essential way of relieving stress and anxiety. Children whose lives involve too much work and not enough play significantly lose out in this regard; he believed this to be very serious for their psychological health.

Psycho-social theories of personality development

Erikson's theory of personality development

Erik Erikson (1968) believed that throughout the lifespan, people are faced at different stages with various 'crises' that require resolving. If the 'crisis' is successfully resolved, then a life-stage virtue is achieved; if not, then the person suffers emotional distress. Erikson believed there are eight psychosocial stages (after his death, his wife later added a ninth stage), as follows.

1. **Hope:** Basic trust vs. mistrust (zero to two years). During this stage, the infant basically learns to see the world generally as either a safe and predictable or unsafe and unpredictable place. This stage is closely linked with attachment theory, as described above – does the child believe its caregivers are reliable?

2. **Will:** Autonomy vs. shame and doubt (two to four years). Child needs to learn to explore the world. If parents are too smothering or completely neglectful, the child will develop self-doubt and be unsure of or ashamed of their abilities.

3. **Purpose:** Initiative vs. guilt (four to six years). Can the child plan or do things on his or her own, such as dress him or herself? If 'guilty' about making his or her own choices, the child will not function well. Erikson has a positive outlook on this stage, saying that most guilt is quickly compensated by a sense of accomplishment.

4. **Competence:** Industry vs. inferiority (around age six to puberty). Child comparing self-worth to others (such as a classmate). Child can recognise major disparities in personal abilities relative to other children. Erikson places some emphasis on the teacher, who should ensure that children do not feel inferior.

5. **Fidelity:** Identity vs. role confusion (11 to 19 years). Questioning of self. Who am I, how do I fit in? Where am I going in life? Erikson believes that if parents allow the child to explore, they will conclude their own identity. However, if the parents continually push him or her to conform to their views, e.g. a doctor insisting her son also does medicine, the adolescent will face identity confusion.

6. **Love:** Intimacy vs. isolation (19 to 40 years). Who do I want to be with or date, what am I going to do with my life? Will I settle down? This stage has begun to last longer as young adults choose to stay in school and not settle as early as in years gone by.

7. **Caring:** Generativity vs. stagnation (40 to 64 years). Individual measures accomplishments/failures. Am I satisfied or not? The need to assist the younger generation. Stagnation is the feeling of not having done anything positive with one's life, especially to help the next generation.

8. **Wisdom:** Ego integrity vs. despair (65+ years). Some handle death well. Some can be bitter, unhappy and dissatisfied with what they have accomplished or failed to accomplish within their lifetime. They reflect on the past and either feel satisfaction or despair.

Implications of Erikson's theory for those caring for children

Erikson's first three stages are most relevant to people working and caring for young children. The following points are important.

*   Children in childcare settings should have a key worker, someone they can form a close bond with and can rely on.

- It is important for children's emotional well-being that crèches and preschools do not have a high staff turnover or high rates of staff absenteeism. Owners need to ensure that childcare staff are well treated and adequately paid to encourage loyalty. This can make quality childcare expensive. Parents need to realise this.
- Children should be encouraged to do things for themselves, e.g. spoon feed. Sometimes crèches, in the interests of speed and keeping children's clothing clean, do too much for children. This is not desirable for development. Likewise, parents should not expect children to come back from daycare as clean as they went into it.
- Childcare staff should set tasks and activities at the correct level for children so that the child has a reasonable chance of succeeding at the activity with only a small amount of adult guidance. Avoid over-helping children.

Self-esteem and self-concept

Both self-esteem and self-concept have wide-reaching implications for children's development. **Self-esteem** is defined as a person's general evaluation of themselves, e.g. I am a good person. **Self-concept** is how a person sees themselves in specific areas, e.g. am I attractive looking? Am I good at sports? Am I good academically? etc. Both concepts are closely linked. People's self-esteem and self-concepts may not be accurate. For example, a child with low self-esteem may see themselves as unattractive, academically weak and bad at sports (negative self-concepts), even though they are not any of these things.

Measuring self-esteem

One of the best-known tools for measuring self-esteem is a 10-item questionnaire developed by Morris Rosenburg in 1965. It is still being used today (see below).

1 = strongly agree, 2 = agree, 3 = disagree, 4 = strongly disagree				
Item	**1**	**2**	**3**	**4**
1. On the whole, I am satisfied with myself				
2. At times, I think I am no good at all				
3. I feel I have a number of good qualities				
4. I am able to do things as well as most other people				
5. I feel I do not have much to be proud of				
6. I certainly feel useless at times				
7. I feel that I'm a person of worth, at least on an equal plane with others				
8. I wish I could have more respect for myself				

Item	1	2	3	4
9. All in all, I am inclined to feel that I am a failure				
10. I take a positive attitude towards myself				

Scoring the questionnaire

- For questions 1, 3, 4, 7 and 10: 1 = 1 point, 2 = 2 points, 3 = 3 points and 4 = 4 points
- For questions 2, 5, 6, 8 and 9: 1 = 4 points, 2 = 3 points, 3 = 2 points and 4 = 1 point

Scores below 15 suggest low self-esteem

For younger children, measures such as Susan Harter's Self-Perception Profile for Children (1985) have been used. This particular tool is designed to be used with children between approximately six to 10 years and looks at five areas: perceived physical appearance, scholastic (academic) competence, social acceptance, behavioural conduct and athletic competence. Of these, a child's perception of their physical appearance is most closely linked with self-esteem.

Increasing children's self-esteem

Today, two main problems or issues arise in relation to children's self-esteem: the old one, whereby children are not given sufficient recognition and praise for their efforts and are instead frequently run down and criticised, and the new one, whereby children are praised anyway, even if what they do is an effortless, mediocre or even a poor attempt.

Both of these situations can cause self-esteem issues for children. Children in the first situation may grow up with low self-esteem, while children in the second situation may grow up with inflated self-esteem, unable to cope effectively with competition or criticism.

In order to promote self-esteem, it is important not to offer blanket, undeserved praise. Children have good levels of self-esteem when they perform well in areas important to them. Children should therefore be encouraged to identify their areas of strength and work on them. For example, a child who is not very good at sports but is good musically should be encouraged and praised for joining the local brass band. He or she should be helped and encouraged to practise to achieve a good level of competence so that he or she is appreciated by other band members, thus raising self-esteem.

How Aistear promotes emotional development

Promotion of children's emotional development is at the very heart of the Aistear curriculum framework. It advocates:

- Celebrating each child's uniqueness.

- Treating each child equally and with respect.
- Appreciating and valuing diversity, e.g. culture, region, language.
- Respecting children as citizens.
- Helping children feel secure in the setting by forming close relationships with the home environment.
- Allowing children to learn through active hands-on experiences – thus giving children a sense of achievement and confidence in their own abilities.
- Listening to children carefully, respecting what they have to say.
- Using positive discipline techniques to help children monitor and guide their own behaviour.
- Allowing children to express their emotions through creative and physical activities.
- Observing children's development (including emotional) in the setting and putting developmentally appropriate interventions in place as required.
- Praising and encouraging children's efforts.

Sample observation

Observation 5: Emotional development

Date of observation: 13 December 2013

Time observation started and finished: 09.00–12.30

Number of children present: 10

Number of adults present: 3 – 2 staff and 1 student (observer)

Permission obtained from: Supervisor

Description of setting: This observation took place during the morning session in a large, private, purpose-built crèche in an urban setting. It caters for children from six months to school-going age and also provides an after-school service. The crèche is open from 8 a.m. to 6 p.m., Monday to Friday, and caters for up to 65 children at a time. Groups are divided according to age – babies, wobblers, toddlers, preschool and after-school. Each group has their own purpose-built room. There is a large all-female staff.

Immediate context: This observation took place during the morning session in the wobbler room. This is a large airy room with plenty of colourful toys. There is a separate sleep room attached. The room can accommodate a total of 10 children and there are 10 in today. This is generally the case – there are six children who are here every day and four others who rotate depending on what day it is.

Brief description of the child observed: TC is a female aged 22 months. She is large for her age and very active. TC's mother has recently had twin boys (they are now three months old).

TC has continued in the crèche during her mother's maternity leave. While TC's passive vocabulary is extensive, her active vocabulary is limited and she uses only a few words at present. In recent weeks, TC has developed a tendency to be quite rough with the other children. She tends to push, grab and pull toys off them as well as hit and bite.

Aim of observation: The aim of this observation is to observe TC during the morning session in order to assess her emotional development.

Rationale: In recent weeks, TC has begun behaving in an unacceptable manner towards the other children in the room. She pushes other children, pulls toys off them, frequently hits out and sometimes bites. Staff members are concerned about this and wish to observe TC in order to assess what is triggering this behaviour and how it is being dealt with.

Method: Event sample

Media used: Pen, prepared event sample grid, clipboard

Date	Time	P/UP	Antecedent	Description of behaviour	Consequence
13/12	9.22	UP	Child L was sitting alone playing with shape sorter on floor.	TC walks over to child L and pulls the shape sorter off her. Child L stands up and tries to resist. TC pushes her and she falls back to the floor. Child L begins to cry.	A walks over and takes shape sorter from TC, saying, 'Don't push, you have to wait till child L is finished, TC.' TC jumps up and down shouting 'no' and then lies face down on the floor, crying.
13/12	10.19	UP	Three children are playing with Duplo on the floor.	TC sits with three other children. Shortly after joining them, she begins to scatter and throw the Duplo.	A goes over and says 'No, don't throw the bricks, TC, you could hit someone and hurt them.' A puts the Duplo back in pile the children are playing with and takes TC with her by the hand. TC resists, saying 'no'. A lets go of TC in a few minutes and she returns to blocks.
13/12	10.21	P	Child M says, 'No, TC, go away,' and pushes her away from Duplo.	TC begins fighting with child M, pinching her face.	A walks quickly over and says, 'No, TC, that is not nice, you have to sit on the bold mat.' TC says, 'No, no, no.' A takes TC by the hand to the bold mat and tries to get TC to sit on it. TC begins to cry and will not stay on the mat. A stays with TC until she has calmed down. A says, 'You can't pinch, you must not pinch, no no, that's bold, TC.'

13/12	11.00	UP	The children are having their snack around a large round table. Ham sandwiches with juice.	TC begins sticking her fingers into child O's sandwich.	A says, 'No, TC, don't do that, child O wants to eat that.' A moves TC over beside her.
13/12	11.15	UP	Child N is playing with a doll and pram. She is pretending the doll is asleep.	TC walks up to child N and tries to pull the pram off child N as she appears to want to push it round the room. Child N resists and TC bites her (lightly) on the arm where she is holding the pram. Child N cries loudly.	A walks over immediately to child N and begins to comfort her. A second adult comes over and speaks loudly to TC, 'That is very, very bold, TC, you never, never bite, you have hurt child N, that's very bold, TC.' A walks away with TC and another staff member comforts child N.
13/12	12.06	UP	Two children together with TC are at the water play area.	TC begins fighting over a blue plastic jug with child L. Child L resists, saying 'no'. TC pulls harder and gets the cup off child L, then starts to hit child L with it on the arm.	A takes the cup off TC and says, 'That's not nice, TC, now away from the water.' A takes TC away from the water. TC resists, sitting on the ground, crying. A persists in taking TC over, saying, 'We need to do your nappy, TC.'

Note: P/UP means provoked or unprovoked.

Evaluation

(See Chapter 4, p. 93 for a note on the structure of evaluations.)

The aim of this observation was to observe TC over the course of the morning in order to assess her emotional development. I feel that this aim was achieved very well as TC was observed very closely over a full morning and all incidents accurately and objectively recorded. TC's behaviour of late has been causing some concern in that she seems to be frequently pushing other children, pulling toys off them, hitting out and sometimes even biting them. This observation seeks to observe how often this behaviour does actually occur, what, if anything, is triggering it and also how TC's behaviour is being dealt with by staff.

Over the course of the morning, TC is engaged in a total of five incidents where she wants something another child has and tries to take it by force. Piaget believed that children under the age of two are cognitively egocentric in that they find it difficult to see something from another person's perspective. This could explain why TC does not seem to take the feelings of her peers into account, e.g. pulling the shape sorter off child L, pinching child M, biting and pulling the pram off child N and taking the blue plastic jug off child L. Having said this, at the minute TC does seem to behave like this more than the other children in the room who are all the same age. This could be TC's emotional response to her mother recently having twin boys, taking her emotional confusion out on the children in the crèche.

Staff for the most part respond to TC's behaviour from a care perspective:

In addition, it is important that preschools and schools advocate a care perspective for the promotion of moral development. Such a perspective concentrates on educating children about the importance of engaging in pro-social behaviours such as considering the feelings of others, being sensitive to the needs of others and helping each other…

(Flood 2013)

Examples of where staff use a care perspective in this observation are when TC throws the bricks, the staff member says, 'No, don't throw bricks, TC, you could hit someone and hurt them.' Another example is when TC bites child N and the staff member says, 'That is very, very bold, TC, you never, never bite, you have hurt child N, that is very bold, TC.'

Having said this, the language staff use towards TC is somewhat negative, e.g. 'That's bold, you will have to go on the bold mat,' and so on. Perhaps staff could say something like 'No TC, biting hurts, we never bite.'

Hoffman (1970) suggests that induction should be used as a discipline technique with children. This is where the adult reasons with the child and explains the consequences of his or her actions. Induction is similar to the care perspective described above. Induction, while it was used during this observation, was not always used. At times a more behaviourist approach (punishment) was used, such as when TC was made to sit on the bold mat or when the adult speaks loudly to TC after she bit child N. This could be because TC is quite young and perhaps staff felt she may not understand them if a short, simple message was not given.

TC's language is quite limited. During this observation her responses were limited to single words, e.g. 'no'. This may be one of the reasons why TC is acting the way she is. If TC is angry, jealous or confused about the situation at home, she is not able to express her emotions through words and is therefore acting out instead. Of course, this may not be the reason for her actions. It is not possible to tell for sure because she cannot speak yet for herself.

In summary, TC does seem to be angry and frustrated at the minute. This could be as a result of the recent changes in her family structure and the inevitable reduction in the amount of attention she is getting there. Staff in the crèche are for the most part dealing with TC's behaviour from an appropriate care perspective and using induction as a discipline technique.

Personal learning

- I learned how important it is to objectively observe children to get an accurate picture of what is actually happening in the childcare setting.
- I learned that when children act in a way that hurts or may hurt others, adults should adopt a care perspective and use induction as a discipline technique. This way, the child learns to consider things from someone else's point of view.
- I learned that language helps emotional expression and that while their language skills are still developing, children may act out their emotions.

Recommendations

- Perhaps it is not a good idea to use negative language like 'That is bold' with young children. It might be better to word things in a positive way, e.g. 'We must be nice.' Although with something as serious as biting it is understandable that staff feel the need to be stern with TC.
- Staff must watch TC carefully while she is going through this emotional time as it is not acceptable for her to hurt other children in the setting. Staff should however be careful not to treat TC in an overly negative way.
- Perhaps staff could make time to spend on one-to-one activities with TC. The fact that her mother has just had twin boys probably means that TC is not now getting the attention she was used to at home and may be feeling a little left out.

References

Flood, E. (2013), *Child Development for Students in Ireland* (2nd edn.). Dublin: Gill & Macmillan.

Hoffman, M. (1970), 'Moral Development', in M. Bornstein (ed.), *Manual of Child Psychology* (3rd edn., Vol. 2). New York: Wiley.

Signatures

Jenny Sheridan   Date: <u>13/12/2013</u>
Student

Lisa Gibson   Date: <u>13/12/2013</u>
Supervisor

Sarah Tuite   Date: <u>14/01/2013</u>
Tutor

Revision questions

1. Define emotional development.
2. What is separation distress? When does it generally peak?
3. What is emotional regulation? How does children's ability in this area emerge?
4. What bearing could infant temperament have on emotional development?
5. In relation to parenting, what is meant by 'goodness of fit'?
6. Outline Bowlby's attachment theory.
7. Describe how Mary Ainsworth (1979) studied the differences in the quality of babies' attachments to their mothers.
8. Do you think her results would be valid today?
9. What significance do you think Harry Harlow's studies of maternal deprivation have for human emotional development?
10. Evaluate attachment theory.
11. Briefly outline Freud's theories of emotional development.
12. Briefly outline each of the following theorists' theories of emotional development: (a) Anna Freud, (b) Melanie Klein, (c) D.W. Winnicott. (FETAC Level 6 only)
13. By six years of age, children have passed through three of Erikson's psychosocial stages. Outline these three stages.
14. What implications does Erikson's theory of personality development have for those caring for children?
15. Define self-esteem and self-concept.
16. How is children's self-esteem best promoted?

CHAPTER NINE

Assessment of Child Development Modules (Levels 5 and 6)

Level 5 – Child Development 5N1764

There are three elements to the assessment of this module.

Part 1:   Collection of work (40%) – 5 observations

Part 2:   Assignment (30%) – Play activity or experience

Part 3:   Written examination (30%)

This chapter offers a sample brief for each piece of work listed above, together with suggested guidelines. It must be emphasised however that students should follow exactly the brief given by their particular college as there may be some differences in interpretation. Copies of briefs and a sample examination is available on the teachers' CD that accompanies this book.

Part 1: Collection of work (40%)
Sample brief

Child Development (5N1764)
Collection of Work (40%)

The Collection of Work will include five child observations. A minimum of three methods/techniques must be used by you in compiling the collection of work. Each observation must address one of the five areas of development, i.e. Physical, Cognitive, Social,

Emotional and Language. Each of the following age ranges will be represented in at least one observation; 0–1 years, 1–3 years, 3–6 years. You are required to present written documentation in support of each observation. The written documentation will consist of the following sections:

1. **Aim:** A statement on the aim, objectives and rationale of the observation clearly stating which area of development is being observed. (5 x 1 mark)

2. **Background information:** Details of the setting. The type of observation method/technique used. The time of starting and finishing the observation. The date of the observation. A brief description of the child/group of children including age, gender and any other relevant details. (5 x 1 mark)

3. **Observation record:** An objective account of the observation. Format will depend on the observation method/technique used, e.g. checklist, time sample, event sample, anecdotal record, narrative/written record etc. (5 x 4 marks)

4. **Evaluation:** An explanation of the data. Integration with previous learning and experience. Inclusion of relevant citations. The candidate will demonstrate sensitivity to the needs of the individual children and their development and also to the limitations of normative measurement. (5 x 2 marks)

5. **Recommendations:** Make recommendations of appropriate ways to meet the developmental needs of the child. (5 x 2 marks)

6. **Personal learning:** A reflection by the candidate on their own understanding of child development and any other incidental learning they have realised from doing this observation. (5 x 1 mark)

Specified range of developmental areas and ages studied (20 marks)

Required number of methods/techniques employed (5 marks)

Due date: _____

Date of submission: _____

This is my own work. Signature of student: _____

Signature of tutor: _____

Guidelines

Guidelines for observations are provided in Chapter 3 and also at the end of each development chapter where there is a sample observation concerning that area of development.

Part 2: Assignment (30%) – Play Activity/Experience
Sample brief

Child Development (5N1764)
Assignment (30%)

For this assignment you are required to plan, implement, evaluate and make recommendations with regards to a developmentally appropriate and beneficial play activity/experience for a child or group of children. You are required to present evidence of:

1. Observation of the child/children prior to planning the activity in order to assess their development and learning needs. (5 marks)
2. Planning of the activity. (4 marks)
3. Implementation of the activity. (2 marks)
4. Evaluation of the impact of the play activity on the child/children's development and learning with reference to relevant research/theory. (15 marks)
5. Recommendations regarding how the activity could be (a) better planned and/or implemented and (b) followed up on with future activities. (4 marks)
6. Evaluation of your role in supporting the needs of the child/children with reference to relevant research/theory. (15 marks)
7. Explanation and evaluation of how your chosen play activity links to Aistear's four themes, i.e. well-being, identity and belonging, communication, exploring and thinking. (15 marks)

Due date: _____

Date of submission: _____

This is my own work. Signature of student: _____

Signature of tutor: _____

Guidelines

1. Observation of the child/children prior to planning the activity in order to assess their development and learning needs. (5 marks)

For this part of the assignment you need to carry out one observation which looks at your target child or children's holistic development. It is probably easiest to carry out an observation using the narrative method as this method is suitable for observing all areas of development, i.e. physical, intellectual/cognitive, language, social and emotional. A sample of this type of observation is given towards the end of Chapter 5.

This observation will be a little different from the one in Chapter 5, however, in that you are going focus on the holistic development of the child or children, not just on one single area of development (as you did for your collection of work). Your aim will therefore be broader, e.g. 'I aim to observe TC's overall development over a period of ten minutes using the narrative method.' Your rationale will relate to the rest of this assignment, e.g. 'I am carrying out this observation in order to plan a suitable play activity for TC that best meets her needs.'

2. Planning of the activity (4 marks)

Here you should introduce your activity with an aim, objectives and a rationale. You should then describe how you planned your activity. Explain how you consulted with an adult in a supervisory role before undertaking the activity; mention any advice or guidance you were given. What preparations did you make, what equipment did you gather? Under Planning outline any health and safety factors that you had to investigate or consider.

3. Implementation (2 marks)

Here you describe in a step-by-step fashion how you plan to carry out the activity. For students starting out this is an important step. Writing out the implementation like this will alert you to any factors that you need to consider, e.g. extra equipment required etc.

4. Evaluation (15 marks)

This section is worth a lot of marks, therefore it should be done to the best of your ability. As with any evaluation – the following structure should be followed:

First paragraph – Introduction

- Restate the aim of your activity.
- State whether you think your aim was achieved and generally why you think this.
- If there was anything that went particularly badly mention it here also.

Middle three or four paragraphs

Make three or four strong points regarding how the activity actually went. Each point you make should be backed up with a piece of theory or research.

Example

The children were shown three sample Christmas cards. Resources for all three cards were laid out on the table so children were free to make whichever one they liked best. Four of the children chose the same card (the Christmas pudding card), one chose the Christmas tree card and the other chose the Christmas stocking card. I feel that because children could choose what they wished to make they were highly motivated by the activity. William Glasser (in Flood 2013) is a firm believer in giving choices to children in schools and pre-schools and this is a key concept of his choice theory.

Last paragraph – conclusion

(a) Restate your aim, (b) restate whether you feel it was achieved or not, and (c) briefly recap on the main points of your evaluation (yes, this is repetitive, but is generally how a conclusion is written).

5. Recommendations regarding how the activity could be (a) better planned and/or implemented, and (b) followed up on with future activities. (4 marks)

In this section you should make *specific* recommendations. Good marks will not be awarded for general statements, e.g. I could have planned the activity better. Be specific.

6. Evaluation of your role in supporting the needs of the child/children with reference to relevant research/theory. (15 marks)

Again there is a substantial number of marks going for this section. You should structure this evaluation much as you did the evaluation in part 4 above. Be sure to refer to theory. Ask yourself what characteristics of a good early years' practitioner did you display while carrying out this activity? Also of course outline any areas where you feel you could improve. You should also mention Vygotsky – scaffolding and children's Zone of Proximal Development (ZPD – see Chapter 5) – or any other theorist you feel is relevant.

7. Explanation and evaluation of how your chosen play activity links to Aistear's four themes, i.e. well-being, identity and belonging, communication, exploring and thinking. (15 marks)

For this section you need to download and read Aistear's principles and themes booklet – www.ncca.biz/Aistear. The sections on Aistear towards the end of Chapters 4–8 of this book may also be of assistance. You need to pick out relevant themes, aims and learning goals within this document and explain and evaluate in detail how your activity helps achieve these themes, aims and learning goals.

Note: As with all assignments you normally include a title page and table of contents. You also need to include evidence that you actually carried out the activity, for example:

- A signed statement by your workplace supervisor.
- Photos (you will need to get permission for this and children's faces should *not* be shown).
- Samples of children's work – no surnames should be written on the work.

Part 3: Written examination (30%)

The written examination consists of 10 short questions (you must answer all 10) and two longer structured questions (you must answer both). The revision questions at the end of each chapter in this book will help you prepare for this examination.

Teachers: A sample examination is given on the CD accompanying this book.

Level 6 – Child Development 6N1942

There are **two** elements to the assessment of this module.

Part 1: Project (60%)

Part 2: Written Examination (40%)

This section offers a sample brief for the project together with suggested guidelines. It must be emphasised however that students should follow exactly the brief given by their particular college as there may be some differences in interpretation. A sample brief and examination paper is available on the teachers' CD that accompanies this book.

Part 1: project (60%)

Sample brief

Child Development (6N1942) Collection of Work (60%)

For this project you are required to work with a child or a group of children over an extended period of time on an intervention or series of interventions designed to promote an aspect or aspects of their development. The project should include:

1. Title page.
2. Table of contents.
3. Aim, objectives and rationale for the project.
4. Evidence that the child/children have been extensively observed over a period of time.

5. Evidence of collaboration with relevant stakeholders with regards to (a) your observations of the child/children and also (b) your plans for intervention with the child/children.
6. Comprehensive intervention plan(s).
7. Detailed plans for each intervention(s), to include:
   (a) Aim, objectives and rationale.
   (b) Details of planning.
   (c) Details of step-by-step intervention.
   (d) Description of how intervention/s went.
   (e) Evaluation and reflection on the effectiveness of intervention/s.
   (f) Recommendations for future work with the child/children.
8. Overall evaluation.
9. Overall recommendations.
10. References.

Due date: _____

Date of submission: _____

This is my own work. Signature of student: _____

Signature of tutor: _____

Guidelines

3. Aim, objectives and rationale

An aim is a broad statement outlining what you hope to achieve with this project. For example, 'The aim of this project is to work with a child or a group of children over an extended period of time on an intervention or series of interventions designed to promote an aspect or aspects of their development.'

Objectives: Provide detailed information on what you intend to do to achieve your aim. For example: 'To discuss this project with my supervisor and make a plan with her for carrying out a series of observations and a number of developmentally appropriate activities with a small group of children in the setting.' Your list of objectives should include all the requirements outlined in the brief.

Rationale: Provide reasons why this is an appropriate and worthwhile piece of work to carry out in the setting.

4. Evidence that the child/children have been extensively observed over a period of time.

You must carry out a series of observations on the child or children you have planned to carry out the intervention activity/activities with. It is good practice to adopt a holistic approach and carry out at least one observation on all five areas of development. If there is a particular area of concern or interest, e.g. a child's language development, you should carry out more than one observation in this area. You should write up your observations based on the sample observations given towards the end of Chapters 4–8 in this book.

5. Evidence of collaboration with relevant stakeholders with regards to (a) your observations of the child/children and also (b) your plans for intervention with the child/children.

You should have a series of meetings with your workplace supervisor or any other relevant stakeholder regarding this project. Minutes of these meetings should be recorded as evidence of this collaboration. The minutes should be signed by you and also any relevant stakeholders, e.g. your supervisor.

6. Comprehensive intervention plan(s) with rationale for each one.

You must make a record of your planned activities. Record what intervention activities you are going to carry out and when (see table below).

Sample Intervention plan – playing traditional playground games with a group of children to help increase their physical fitness

Planned intervention activity	Proposed date for activity
Hopscotch	9 January 2014
Skipping (long rope, two adults holding)	16 January 2014
Donkey	23 January 2014

7. Detailed plans for each intervention(s), to include:
  (a) Aim, objectives and rationale.
  (b) Details of planning.
  (c) Details of step-by-step intervention.
  (d) Description of how intervention/s went.
  (e) Evaluation and reflection on the effectiveness of intervention/s.
  (f) Recommendations for future work with the child/children.

8. Overall evaluation.

Here you must evaluate the whole project. This evaluation could be structured thus:

First paragraph
• Restate the overall aim of the project and its rationale.
• State whether you feel the overall aim was achieved. Give a broad statement of why you think it was/wasn't achieved.

Middle three or four paragraphs

Here you make three or four important points relating to your project. Relate each point you make to theory or a statistic. You should use one paragraph to show how your chosen intervention(s) relate to Aistear.

Example

'Through my observations of children in the pre-school room I found that on a daily basis the children rarely get the opportunity to play outside – over the course of the five Fridays I spent observing, they had only been out once. This is why I chose a series of outdoor activities for my planned interventions. Growing up in Ireland (1997), the government-sponsored longitudinal study of children in Ireland, found that 22 per cent of Irish boys and 30 per cent of Irish girls were overweight or obese at nine years of age. This is a very frightening statistic. I felt that it would be a good idea to introduce children in my pre-school to some of the traditional games I played at school as a child. My supervisor (who also remembers these games) thought it was a great idea and fully supported me.'

Final paragraph – conclusion

Here you restate your aim, restate what the main findings of your observations where, restate what your chosen interventions were and finally restate very briefly how you feel the interventions benefited the children involved.

Overall recommendations

Here you must give a number (three or four) of targeted recommendations for (a) how you could improve this project were you to do it again, and (b) how this work could be extended and developed in the future.

References

Please see Appendix 1 for guidelines on referencing.

Written Examination (40%)

The examination consists of six structured questions; you must answer four. The revision questions at the end of each chapter in this book will help you prepare for this examination.

Teachers: A sample examination is given on the CD accompanying this book.

Appendix 1: Referencing and Bibliography

Quoting directly from books

- If you are quoting directly from a source, e.g. textbook, you must quote word for word, enclosing the quote with quotation marks. However, if you are only using a line or two, then you can blend it into your own text. Example:

  In my observation, TC took four short steps from the activity table to the bean bag. This is usual for this age group, as 'when infants learn to walk, they typically take small steps because of their limited balance control and strength' (Santrock 2009: 158).

- If you are quoting a large passage of text, then it should be presented as a block quote on its own. It should be indented to make it stand out. A block quote does not need quotation marks. If you do not quote a sentence in full, indicate this by using an ellipsis (…). Example:

  The motor accomplishments of the first year bring increasing independence, allowing infants to explore their environment more extensively and to initiate interactions with others more readily … (Santrock 2009: 159)

- If you wish to mention the author's name as part of your own sentence but not quote them directly, this is called a citation. Example:

  Santrock (2009) believes that because infants have limited balance control and strength, they typically take small steps while learning to walk.

- Practices differ on this, but if a text has more than three authors, then in the text you can use et al., such as Beaver et al. (1999). However, all the authors should be listed in the references at the back.

Creating a reference list at the back of your report

References should be written in alphabetical order.

Books

In the reference section, the full reference for the books you have taken quotes or citations from should be written as follows:

1. Author surname
2. Author initial
3. Year of publication
4. Title (in italics); state which edition if applicable
5. Place of publication
6. Name of the publisher.

The placement of commas, full stops, brackets and italics are all important. Example:

Santrock, J. (2009), *Child Development* (12th edn.). New York: McGraw-Hill Companies Inc.

Journals

Journal articles should be written as follows:

1. Author surname
2. Author initial
3. Year of publication
4. Title of journal article (in quotation marks)
5. Name of journal (in italics)
6. Volume number
7. Issue number (if applicable)
8. Page numbers

Example:

DeCasper, A. and Spence, M. (1986), 'Prenatal Maternal Speech Influences Newborn's Perception of Speech Sounds', *Infant Behaviour and Development*, 9, 133–50.

Collections of work with editor(s)

Sometimes an editor compiles work by a number of different authors. This is referenced as follows:

1. Editor's surname
2. Editor's initial with (ed.) after it
3. Year of publication
4. Title (in italics); state which edition if applicable
5. Place of publication
6. Name of publisher

Example:

Wetherell, M. (ed.) (1996), *Identities, Groups and Social Issues.* London: Sage Publications.

Electronic sources (primarily websites)

Give the full website address, e.g. www.lalecheleagueireland.com (a breastfeeding support and information website).

References

Ainsworth, M. (1979), 'Infant-Mother Attachment', *American Psychologist*, 34, 932–7.

Asperger Syndrome Association of Ireland (2009), *Development Plan 2007–2010*, <www.aspireireland.ie/Documents/Development%20Plan%2007-10.pdf>, accessed 11 November 2012.

Bandura, A. (1977), *Social Learning Theory*. New York: General Learning Press.

Bauer, P. (2007), *Remembering the Times of Our Lives*. Mahwah, NJ: Erlbaum.

Bell, S. and Ainsworth, M. (1972), 'Infant Crying and Responsiveness', *Child Development*, 43, 1171–90.

Berko, J. (1958), 'The Child's Learning of English Morphology', *Word*, 14, 145–69.

Blurton-Jones, N.G. and Konner, M.J. (1973), 'Sex Differences in Behaviour of London and Bushman children', in D.E. Papalia and S. Wendkos Olds, *Human Development* (7th Edn.). USA: McGraw-Hill.

Bouchard, T., Lykken, D., McGue, M., Segal, N. and Tellegen, A. (1990), 'Source of Human Psychological Differences: The Minnesota Study of Twins Reared Apart', *Science*, 250, 223–8.

Bowlby, J. (1958), 'The Nature of the Child's Tie to His Mother', *International Journal of Psychoanalysis*, 39, 350–73.

Bowlby, J. (1969), *Attachment and Loss* (Vol. 1). London: Hogarth Press.

Campbell, M. and Mottola, M. (2001), 'Recreational Exercise and Occupational Safety during Pregnancy and Birth Weight: A Case Control Study', *American Journal of Obstetrics and Gynaecology*, 184, 403–8.

Clark, E. (1993), *The Lexicon in Acquisition*. New York: Cambridge University Press.

Collins, W. and van Dulmen, M. (2006), 'The Significance of Middle Childhood Peer Relationships in Early Adulthood', in A. Huston and M. Ripke (eds.), *Developmental Contexts in Middle Childhood*. New York: Cambridge University Press.

Damon, W. (1988), *The Moral Child*. New York: Free Press.

DeCasper, A. and Spence, M. (1986), 'Prenatal Maternal Speech Influences Newborn's Perception of Speech Sounds', *Infant Behaviour and Development*, 9, 133–50.

Deer, B. (2009), 'MMR Doctor Andrew Wakefield Fixed Data on Autism', *Sunday Post*, 8 February.

Department of Health (2010), 'The Irish Health Behaviour in School Aged Children Study', <www.dohc.ie/publications/hbsc_report.html>, accessed 15 November 2012.

Diamond, A.D. (2007), 'Interrelated and Interdependent', *Developmental Science*, 10, 152–8.

Donaldson, M. (1978), *Children's Minds*. London: Fontana.

Donaldson, M. and Hughes, M. (1978) in The Open University (2006), *Media Kit*, ED209: Child Development DVD-ROM (Media Kit Part 1, Video Band 1). Milton Keynes: The Open University.

Dunn, J. (2007), 'Siblings and Socialisation', in J.E. Grusec and P.D. Hastings (eds.), *Handbook of Socialization*. New York: Guilford.

Erikson, E. (1968), *Identity: Youth and Crisis*. London: Faber.

Fantz, R. (1963), 'Pattern Vision in Newborn Infants', *Science*, 140, 296–7.

Farrell, C., McAvoy, H., Wilde, J. and Combat Poverty Agency (2008), *Tackling Health Inequalities – An All-Ireland Approach to Social Determinants*. Dublin: Combat Poverty Agency/Institute of Public Health in Ireland.

Fenson, L., Dale, P., Resnick, S., Bates, E., Thal, D. and Pethick, S.J. (1994), 'Variability in Early Communicative Development', *Monographs of the Society for Research in Child Development*, 59, 74–5.

Fried, P.A. and Smith, A.M. (2001), 'A Literature Review of the Consequences of Prenatal Marihuana Exposure: An Emerging Theme of a Deficiency in Aspects of Executive Function', *Neurotoxicology and Teratology*, 23/1, 1–11.

Gesell, A. (1934), *Infancy and Human Growth*. New York: Macmillan.

Gibbons, J. and Ng, S. (2004), 'Acting Bilingual and Thinking Bilingual', *Journal of Language and Social Psychology*, 23, 4–6.

Gibson, E. and Walk, R. (1960), 'The "visual cliff"', *Scientific American*, 202, 67–71.

Glover, V., Miles, R., Matta, S., Modi, N. and Stevenson, J. (2005), 'Glucocorticoid Exposure in Preterm Babies Predicts Saliva Cortisol Response to Immunization at 4 Months', *Pediatric Research*, 58/6, 1233–7.

Harlow, H. (1958), 'The Nature of Love', *American Psychologist*, 13, 673–85.

Harris, M., Jones, D. and Grant, J. (1983), 'The Non-verbal Context of Mothers' Speech to Infants', *First Language*, 4, 21–30.

Hart, B. and Risley, T.R. (1995), *Meaningful Differences in the Everyday Experience of Young American Children*. New York: Brooks Publishing.

Harter, S. (1985), *Self-perception Profile for Children*. Denver: University of Denver, Department of Psychology.

Hoffman, M. (1970), 'Moral Development', in M. Bornstein (ed.), *Manual of Child Psychology* (3rd edn., Vol. 2). New York: Wiley.

Holt, J. (1983), *How Children Learn* (revised edition). London: Penguin Books.

Irish Autism Action (2012), *What is Autism*, <www.autismireland.ie/about-autism/what-is-autism>, accesed 11 November 2012.

Kagan, J. (1987), 'Perspectives on Infancy', in J. Osofsky (ed.), *Handbook on Infant Development*. New York: Wiley.

Kohlberg, L. (1958), 'The Development of Modes of Thinking and Choices in Years 10 to 16', PhD dissertation, University of Chicago.

Kramer, L. and Radley, C. (1997), 'Improving Sibling Relationships among Young Children: A Social Skills Training Model', *Family Relations*, 46, 237–46.

Labov, W. (1969), *The Study of Nonstandard English*. Washington, DC: National Council of Teachers of English.

Layte, R. and McCrory, C. (2011), 'Growing Up in Ireland – Overweight and Obesity in 9-Year-Olds', <www.growingup.ie/fileadmin/user_upload/documents/Second_Child_Cohort_Reports/Growing_Up_in_Ireland_-_Overweight_and_Obesity_Among_9-Year-Olds.pdf>, accessed 17 November 2012.

Levinson, D. (1978), *The Seasons of a Man's Life*. New York: Knopf.

Maccoby, E. (2007), 'Historical Overview of Socialisation Theory and Research', in J.E. Grusec and P.D. Hastings (eds.), *Handbook of Socialization*. New York: Guilford.

McAvoy (2006), www.combatpoverty.ie.

Minett, P. (2005), *Child Care and Development* (5th edn.). UK: Hodder Arnold.

Minsky, R. (1996), *Psychoanalysis and Gender*. London: Routledge.

National Council for Curriculum and Assessment (2009), *Aistear – The Early Childhood Curriculum Framework, Principles and Themes*. Dublin: NCCA.

National Council for Curriculum and Assessment (2009), *Aistear – The Early Childhood Curriculum Framework, Guidelines for Good Practice*. Dublin: NCCA.

National Standards for Pre-school Services (2010), <www.dohc.ie/publications/national_standards_preschool2010.html>, accessed 10 November 2012.

Nettle, D. (2003), 'Intelligence and Class Mobility in the British Population', *British Journal of Psychology*, 94, 551–61.

O'Moore, A.M. (1997), *Nationwide Study on Bullying Behaviour in Irish Schools*. Dublin: Trinity College.

Piaget, J. (1932), *The Moral Judgement of the Child*. New York: Harcourt Brace Jovanovich.

Piaget, J. and Inhelder, B. (1969), *The Child's Conception of Space*. New York: W.W. Horton.

Pollard, I. (2007), 'Neuropharmacology of Drugs and Alcohol in Mother and Foetus', *Seminars in Foetal and Neonatal Medicine*, 12.

Pressley, M. (2007), 'Achieving Best Practices', in L. Gambrell, L. Morrow and M. Pressley (eds.), *Best Practices in Literacy Instruction*. New York: Guilford.

Rosenberg, M. (1965), *Society and the Adolescent Self-image*. Princeton, NJ: Princeton University Press.

Santrock, J. (2009), *Child Development* (12th edn.). New York: McGraw-Hill.

Schaffer, H. (1996), *Social Development*. Cambridge: Houghton Mifflin.

Shayer, M. and Wylam, H. (1978), 'The Distribution of Piagetian Stages of Thinking in British Middle and Secondary School Children II', *British Journal of Educational Psychology*, 48, 62–70.

Sheridan, M., revised and updated by Sharma, A. and Cockerill, H. (1997), *From Birth to 5 Years* (3rd edn.). UK: Routledge.

Skinner, B.F. (1957), *Verbal Learning*. New York, Appleton-Century-Crofts.

Spohr, H.L., Williams, J. and Steinhausen, H.C. (2007), 'Foetal Alcohol Spectrum Disorders in Young Adulthood', *Journal of Pediatrics*, 150.

Sylva, K. and Lunt, I. (1980), *Child Development*. London: Blackwell Publishing.

Thelen, E. (2000), 'Perception and Motor Development', in A. Kazdin (ed.), *Encyclopedia of Psychology*. Washington, DC and New York: American Psychological Association and Oxford University Press.

Thomas, A. and Chess, S. (1977), *Temperament and Development*. New York: Brunner/Mazel.

Van Meurs, K. (1999), 'Cigarette Smoking, Pregnancy and the Developing Fetus', *Stanford Medical Review*, 1/1, 14–16.

Wentzel, K. and Asher, S. (1995), 'The Academic Lives of Neglected, Rejected, Popular and Controversial Children', *Child Development*, 66, 754–63.

WHO (2005), 'Sickle Cell Anaemia: Report by the Secretariat', <http://apps.who.int/gb/ebwha/pdf_files/WHA59/A59_9-en.pdf>.

WHO (2012), 'Prevalence and Trends of Stunting Among Pre-School Children',
    <www.who.int/nutgrowthdb/publications/stunting1990_2020/en>, accessed 15 November 2012.
Winnicott, D.W., (1973), *The Child, the Family, and the Outside World*. Harmondsworth: Penguin Books.
World Nuclear Association (2009), 'Nuclear Power in the World Today', <www.world-
    nuclear.org/info/inf01.html>.

WEBSITES

http://en.wikipedia.org/wiki/Attention-deficit_hyperactivity_disorder
http://historical-debates.oireachtas.ie/D/0469/D.0469.199610100006.html
www.crisispregnancy.ie
www.cso.ie
www.irishhealth.com
www.oecd.org

Index